Country Roads
~ of ~
IOWA

A Guide Book
from Country Roads Press

Country Roads
~ of ~
IOWA

Loralee Wenger

Illustrated by
Victoria Sheridan

Country Roads Press
CASTINE • MAINE

Country Roads of Iowa
© 1994 by Loralee Wenger. All rights reserved.

Published by Country Roads Press
P.O. Box 286, Lower Main Street
Castine, Maine 04421

Text and cover design by Edith Allard.
Illustrations by Victoria Sheridan.
Typesetting by Camden Type 'n Graphics.

ISBN 1-56626-062-0

Library of Congress Cataloging-in-Publication Data
Wenger, Loralee, 1951–
    Country roads of Iowa / Loralee Wenger ; illustrator,
Victoria Sheridan.
        p.   cm.
    Includes index.
    ISBN 1-56626-062-0 (pbk) : $9.95
    1. Iowa—Tours.   2. Automobile travel—Iowa—
Iowa—Guidebooks.   I. Title.
F619.3.W46   1994
917.7704'33—dc20   94-5644
                                        CIP

Printed in the United States of America.
10   9   8   7   6   5   4   3   2   1

To the People of the Flood of 1993
and
to my parents who love the land and its people

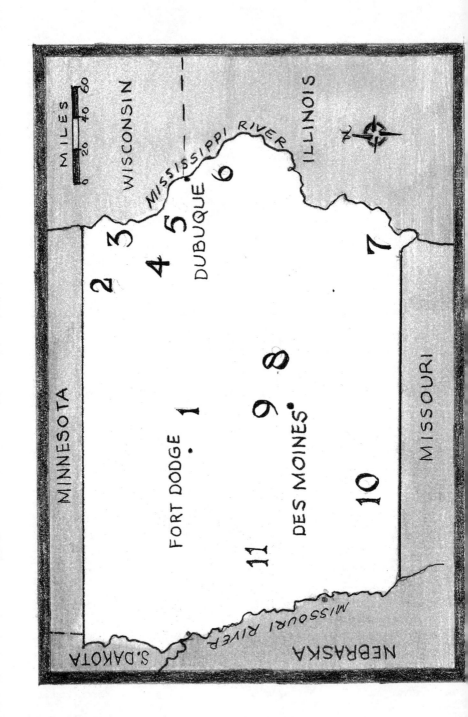

Contents

(& Key to Iowa Country Roads)

Introduction

When I think of country roads, I recall Sunday afternoon rides in the family car and the meandering, graveled, northeast Iowa roads. My mother brought a shovel along to dig up wildflowers. Just seeing her put the shovel in the trunk prompted a groan or a disparaging remark from my father, a farmer, who grumbled that he worked outside all day long and when he rested he wanted the comforts of a house around him. Trees grew thick on both sides of the roads, and flowers lined the shoulders and the ditches. My mother was delighted to find the occasional jack-in-the-pulpit, lady's slipper, or wild honeysuckle.

That was more than twenty-five years ago, and my mother's dream of nurturing a field of wildflowers behind our house never materialized. The wildflowers didn't transplant well. Harsh winters froze them or too much spring rain rotted their roots. My mother has since turned her attention to attracting hummingbirds, which requires no heavy lifting or transplanting, and she and my father are both happier.

Those roads I first explored in our secondhand Plymouth were hilly and winding—a surprise to almost anyone who hasn't lived in that part of Iowa. My mother has taken it upon herself to educate anyone who will listen that all of Iowa isn't flat. As soon as someone says, "Oh, Iowa? That's like South Dakota and Nebraska, isn't it?" or "I've been in Iowa, drove across on I-80 to Chicago once," something in the air changes like a shift in barometric pressure or an electronic impulse about to produce lightning. My mother is about to launch into her soliloquy on OUR part of the state; how, in two words, it's "like Wisconsin" with its hills, winding roads, and trees. Truthfully, a lot of Iowa is flat, but there's a sizeable portion that isn't. I invite you to meander through some of the hilly byways of the northeast as well as eastern, southeastern, and western Iowa.

When I first heard about the Country Roads series, I was excited about writing about my home state. I had been living elsewhere for twenty years, and I wanted to see how Iowa had changed. A friend's reaction—"Country Roads of Iowa, isn't that redundant?"—prompted me to wonder, too. Certainly there were plenty of country roads, but would there be enough alongside them to write about? Although I had visited my home state many times, I had come as a returning daughter. When I visited with the eyes of a traveler, I was pleasantly surprised. The state's residents have had the vision to preserve the once-common-now-historic and the unusual. As Marvin Johnson of Hook's Point Farmstead Bed and Breakfast said, there was a time when most people who didn't live on farms had relatives who did. But for today's city families, there are the Living History Farms, the Midwest Old Threshers' Reunion, the Ploughman Barn at Garber, and the bed-and-breakfast establishments on working farms complete with barns, tractors, woods, creeks, and animals. As usual, I wrote more than was required, and I still left out a lot of interesting routes and places.

If a drive of no particular destination seems almost ludicrous, aimless at best, this is the book for you. I've nosed around and plotted out itineraries. You can follow these routes, selecting the attractions that interest you. On the other hand, if you enjoy poking around, turning on a gravel road just to see where it leads, this book can point out a few general directions, but you're already on your way to serendipity. Whether you travel supplied with carrot sticks and dip as my sister does or with the junk food my brother carries, make the road the journey. Get out of your car, talk with folks, learn something, and have a good time.

Of course this book couldn't have happened the way it did without the help of family and friends. Thanks to Anna Wenger, Gene Wenger, Melinda Wenger Petersen, and Clara Burchett for preliminary research and navigating as I drove around the state. Thanks to my daughter, Elizabeth Wenger Serage, for being a good sport in traveling with me. Thanks to Barbara Wenger, Aaron and Landon Wenger, and Melinda, Adam, and Amy Petersen for traveling with me and entertaining Elizabeth. Special thanks and appreciation to my husband, Jeffrey, for keeping the home fires burning. Thanks to Bonnie and Kent Britten for a lovely reunion and warm hospitality.

Special thanks to Archie Satterfield, author of more than thirty books, and to friends John Mosher and Mary Holscher, who have encouraged me in my writing. And thanks to all of you Iowans who took the time to talk, return phone calls, and answer my letters.

1 ~

Stratford-
Fort Dodge-
West Bend-
Webster
City Loop

From Des Moines: Take I-35 north, and go west on County D65, north on State 17, and west on State 175 to Stratford.

From Waterloo: Take US 20 west, go south on State 17, and west on State 175 to Stratford.

Highlights: *Hook's Point Country Inn, Gardini's General Store in Lehigh, Blue Willow Tea Room at Harcourt, Humboldt County Mill Farm, Fort Dodge Fort Museum and Frontier Village, Grotto of the Redemption, Sod House in West Bend, exotic animal auction in Eagle Grove, 4-H Schoolhouse Museum in Clarion, Dows Mercantile and Train Depot, Bonebright Museum Complex, Centennial Farm Bed and Breakfast. Allow at least two days for this trip.*

When you drive across this flat prairie, it's easy to imagine the sights the early white settlers witnessed—grassy seas shoulder- to head-high stretching, treeless, to the horizon. Those pioneers, full of hope, "tamed" the prairie, busting up the sod and planting it to wheat, corn, and other crops. Eventually they fenced these open lands for grazing. You will find few winding country roads here, as there is little for them to wind around, except the occasional river or stream. Signs for the Dragoon Trail mark the route of Iowa's early military settlement when the Dragoons and then the militia surveyed the territory and established Fort Dodge. In Stratford and Webster

1

City, you can enjoy all the pleasures of "F B&B," farm bed and breakfast, even riding a tractor and gathering eggs for your first meal of the day. In West Bend, adults and children marvel at the multimillion-dollar edifice started by a grateful Roman Catholic priest.

"It's not successful unless they stay past noon and we have a good visit," Marvin Johnson said of his guests at Hook's Point Country Inn northeast of Stratford. (You take County R21 north of town, then go east on Hook's Point Drive to reach the inn. The name Hook's Point comes from the Hook brothers, who settled the area in the late 1840s.) Marvin waits tables, sits on the county's board of supervisors, and, with his two sons, farms 1,800 acres of rich Iowa soil, just like his father, grandfather, and great-grandfather before him. (They weren't waiters, however.) The day I visited, his wife and head chef, Mary Jo, was preparing a gourmet dinner, so Marvin did most of the talking. "Being on a farm is a plus," he said. "It used to be that everyone's grandma and grandpa came from the farm, but that's not true anymore. The barn (built early this century with a hayloft and cupolas) and machine shed are even attractions." Guests thrill to see the 1951 Model B John Deere tractor that he and his sons restored and a surrey complete with fringe on the top. The Johnsons transformed their big red home, nearly all of it original from 1904, into a bed and breakfast in 1987. The house is prairie foursquare architecture, with the same four-room floor plan on each of the two stories. In addition to the three guest rooms decorated with antiques and featherbeds, with advance reservation, Mary Jo serves candlelit, six-course gourmet dinners complete with lace tablecloths and china, three-course luncheons and romantic backwoods picnics, as well as the full farm breakfasts for bed and breakfast guests. She's even served honeymoon couples a private breakfast on her mother's

*There was a time when most people who didn't live on farms
had relatives who did*

wedding china. Guests find no shortage of interesting farm memorabilia, pampering, good food, or conversation here.

After enjoying the farm, head into Stratford for a few hours of shopping and afternoon tea. If you visit in the summer, consider attending the Bluegrass and Old-Time Country Music Festival the second weekend in July at the city park. Many of the shops line Shakespeare Street. Gustafson Glass, the town's stained glass factory, offers its products, gifts, and classes at Glass and Gifts on Shakespeare. Lu's Glass Art produces a range of glassware from delicate Christmas tree ornaments to jewelry and large platters. You will find six rooms of country crafts, candles, and dried flower arrangements at Country Crafts. Antiques are plentiful at Yesteryear Antiques and Cloud's Collectibles, also on Shakespeare Street. For a pleasant pause, try In Good Company, a tea room in a restored early 1900s-era building with pressed tin ceiling and wooden floors where you can enjoy homemade desserts, gourmet coffee, and gifts.

For a pleasant country drive head to Brushy Creek Recreational Area, the largest in the state. (From Stratford, take County R21 north and head west on County D46.) Brushy Creek features 5,800 acres of fields, woods, and valley for hiking and exploring, thirty-five miles of equestrian trails, sixteen miles of snowmobile trails, and 125 campsites. (Continue west on County D46, crossing the Des Moines River to Lehigh.)

A lively pair of Italian sisters, nicknamed Blackie and Sparkie from their high school cheerleading days, run Gardini's General Store, which they have done since 1938. Their parents started the business so that all their five children could work in Lehigh. "It worked, too," said Sparkie, seventy-seven. "The store is kinda' old-fashioned, because it still has the same counters, everything that it did when we started it."

"I guess we're old-fashioned too," she joked, "since we've been here for fifty-five years." Shelves of the small store are stocked with groceries, sewing notions, home canning jars and flats, burlap bags, black buckle overshoes, and more, but it's the sisters who are the draw. "We love to visit with people, and we get all sorts in here," Sparkie said. Between waiting on customers they sew, do needlework and tailoring, and tell jokes. Head south on County P73, which winds along the Des Moines River, then west on State 175 to Harcourt.

The Blue Willow Tea Room and Bakery is one-quarter mile east of Harcourt. You can linger over morning tea or coffee with pastries, enjoy a full scrumptious lunch, or treat yourself to a proper high tea in the afternoon (reservations necessary for high tea). The Tea Room features an elegant but relaxed country decor with wooden beams and a mixture of antique and reproduction oak chairs and lamps. Meals are lovingly presented. Ours featured soup in a small blue-and-white heart-shaped blue crock, a heart-shaped bran muffin with special cream cheese, and the Tea Room's famous chicken salad on a sculptured waffle. Connie Gustafson and her mother-in-law Gwen Gustafson started Country Treasures Gift Shoppe on Gwen's farm in 1975. They added the sixty-seat Tea Room in 1987, naming it after a set of blue willow doll dishes from Connie's childhood. Gwen has since retired, but Connie and a crew keep the operation going. From Harcourt head to Dolliver State Park by taking State 169 north and County D33 east. The park's bluffs, canyons, and Indian mounds offer visual relief from the mostly flat terrain. (Camping also is available there.) Backtrack to I-69 and follow the signs to Fort Dodge.

In 1836 the Dragoons, lightly armed Cavalry soldiers, explored what is now Fort Dodge. Their job was to locate and record the number of American Indians. They had come first

5

to the Keokuk area in 1834; by the spring of 1835 they migrated north to what is now Des Moines, and by August they had reached Fort Dodge. The Dragoon Trail, marked with signs along the highway, winds along the Des Moines River from near Pella up to Webster City and Fort Dodge. Fort Clarke was the original name, but the post was renamed Fort Dodge in honor of Sen. Henry Dodge, territorial governor of the Wisconsin Territory (which included what is now Iowa) and organizer of the Dragoons. White settlers followed the military into the area. They broke the prairie sod for planting crops, and they started early industries of coal mining, railroads, and gypsum mining.

Fort Dodge has had two military posts. The first Fort Dodge, built in 1850, is now on First Avenue North in downtown. Fort Williams, a Civil War fort, was built and staffed by residents in 1862 on Iowa Lake near the Minnesota border. The Fort Museum, US 20 and Museum Road, was patterned after Fort Williams. It features exhibits from Native American settlements, military history, and pioneer times, including period furniture, vintage clothing, and local industry.

We arrived at Fort Dodge during Frontier Days, the first weekend in June. Children clamored around the petting zoo of goats, sheep, and calves, similar to what pioneers may have used to supply milk and cheese. Front Street at the village bustled with activity, resembling that of the early town of Fort Dodge. Boardwalks lead to a blacksmith shop, 1880s jail, newspaper office, drug store, general store, cabinet shop, 1857 school, log chapel, and 1855 log home. Donahoe's General Store sells handcrafted jewelry, hats, coffee mills, brassware, and pottery. At the Sentinel Building, you will find drawers of hand-set type and an antique press. At the blacksmith shop, a smithy uses the anvil, bellows, forge, hammer, and tongs to make horseshoes. At the Ole Fjetland Cabinet Shop, you can see a craftsperson demonstrate old-time hand tools donated by the Byron Fjetland family. The Elkhorn

Creek Cafe is built much like a boom town building with the wood store front and a tent behind it. If there was enough money or if a railroad construction crew came through, wooden walls might be added. As we strolled through tents filled with tables of arts and crafts, my daughter Elizabeth yearned for a hand-crocheted collar made by Pat Garrett of Stuart and a jar of homemade pickles. What a combination!

Women in calico dresses and bonnets tended their iron kettles over campfires. After my nephew Adam saw workers making tools and scraping hides to make soft leather, he bought a piece of supple leather. The children were curious about the pioneers. They watched a tiny girl in a long dress and bonnet help her mother tend the campfire and dry tin plates and cups. At lunchtime, the children were thankful the food stands featured hot dogs instead of fried mush, dandelion greens, or salt pork.

The fort isn't Fort Dodge's only important area. The Blanden Memorial Art Museum, the first permanent city art gallery in the state, is in the Oak Hill Historic District. Founded in 1930, the municipal art museum includes works by local artists; paintings, sculpture, and textiles from Europe and America; as well as African, Asian, and pre-Columbian art. If you're in the mood for something not so ancient as pre-Columbian, visit Old Harvester Gifts and Antiques, 1911 First Avenue North, which has eight rooms of furniture, dishes, baskets, and linens, or try Make Mine Country, 2224 Second Avenue North, six rooms of handmade country crafts, furniture, crocks, candles, and gifts.

If you want to see virgin Iowa prairie, head west from Fort Dodge on State 7, then north on County N65 at Manson to Kalsow Prairie. Otherwise, leave 'Dodge on County P56 north, following the Des Moines River, to Dakota City. On the eastern edge of the little town is the Humboldt County Mill Farm Museum, a complex that includes an 1879 Italianate

mansion, an authentically furnished log cabin, an 1883 one-
room schoohouse, a barn with early farm equipment, and
a collection of Native American artifacts. Continue west
through the town on State 3, backtracking south slightly on
US 169 to Humboldt to Grandma Anna's for an antiques,
crafts, and gifts stop. From Humboldt, zigzag cross-country,
taking State 3 and then county roads C29, P33, C20, P20, and
B63 into West Bend.

The first white settlers in this area came in 1855 and built
houses on the west bend of the Des Moines River. When the
Chicago, Rock Island Railroad came through the area, they
moved four miles east and decided to call their settlement
West Bend. In 1885 a group of Presbyterians built a church
that served the congregation until 1972. The structure now
houses the West Bend Historical Museum, which includes
a pioneer doctor's office, farm equipment, and World War I
artifacts.

Palo Alto County's first schoolhouse, now on State 15 a
block east of the business district, has been preserved. Adjacent to it is a sod house, constructed in much the same way as
the pioneers would have done. The one-room school, built in
1872, was part of the town's original settlement. When the
railroad came through, the school was moved with the rest
of the village. The school was the center for social activities,
and the first church services were held there. Later it was
used as the town's newspaper office. Mrs. Tassie McFarland
Brown, an earlier pupil and the last teacher there, was the
authority in the restoration and arrangement of the furnishings. Beside the school is a sod house like those used by
homesteaders. The sod was inexpensive and good insulation
in a land of few trees. In the 1880s, after the railroad made
shipping lumber inexpensive, sod houses were no longer so
prevalent. Downtown West Bend contains several old brick
buildings, including the Franklin Hotel Mall that is now an
antiques shop.

Sod houses provided a first home for many early settlers

Farther north, just two blocks west of State 15, is the attraction for which West Bend is best known—the Grotto of the Redemption. Father Paul Dobberstein suffered a serious illness as a young man, and he promised that if he recovered he would build a shrine. He started the grotto in 1912 and he worked on it for forty-two years, setting rocks and gems into concrete to create a monument portraying the life of Christ and the fall of humankind and redemption through the way of the cross. The estimated geological value of the work is $2.5 million. When Father Dobberstein died, Father Louis Greving continued construction.

I doubt that the most religious supplicant could be drawn to the grotto more than my five-year-old daughter. Elizabeth listened intently to the tour guide's speech. Over and over, she pulled on my hand to show me a special rock, saying, "Mom, look at THIS." This child, who has her own collection of black, gray, and brown rocks in our backyard, was fascinated with the polished agates, the cut geodes, the sparkling mica, not to mention their arrangement into towering spires, altars, and a maze of narrow walkways, embellished by bells, chimes, and taped music, all surrounding the baby Jesus and Jesus the man.

South of the grotto is St. Peter and Paul's Church, which includes a Christmas Chapel with a 300-pound Brazilian amethyst. The main altar of the church is hand-carved birds-eye maple that won first place at the Chicago World's Fair in 1893. A man-made pond north of the grotto is populated by swans, ducks, and geese in the summer and ice skaters in winter.

After a tour of the grotto, a visit to the church, a walk through the gift shop, and a stroll by the pond, I confess, I resorted to an offer of an ice-cream cone from the shop across the street to get Elizabeth to leave gracefully. Elizabeth gave their ice cream two thumbs up. The adjacent craft shop features pillow cases with hand-crocheted lace edgings and Iowa crafts. From West Bend, backtrack on County P20, County C20, and then south on State 17 and east on State 3 to Goldfield.

One morning, as I cleaned rubbish out of the car, I looked up to see a handful of women briskly walking down the middle of the street. I waved and said hello. They smiled in return, and I overheard one say, "That's Melinda Petersen's sister." Goldfield is the kind of place where I wave to strangers, because I assume they're all my sister's friends. I relaxed on Melinda and her husband Morris's big wrap-around porch, while Elizabeth played with her cousins in their rambling yard. For those of you who don't have relatives in Goldfield, there are a handful of shops to enjoy. Field's Antiques on State 3 features Depression glass, furniture, linens, and collectibles. The Goldfield Cheese Mart and Gift Shop on State 3 sells locally made cheese, LeWright processed meats (from nearby Eagle Grove), candles, crafts, and dolls. You can find handmade designer quilts and pillows from the Native American Dakota Company at Goldfield's Dakota Shop, owned by Maureen Cameron. Her brother, George, helped to start the company when, as a VISTA volunteer, he was given an assignment to develop employment opportunities for Native Americans. He was about to give up when he realized that he was surrounded by native women making artistic designs and expert quilting. The first year, he was laughed out of major department stores; the second year, the company couldn't keep up with the orders. The Dakota Shop also features a gift shop and a tea table. From Goldfield, take State 17 south to Eagle Grove.

This small community holds the distinction of hosting an exotic animal auction twice a year, usually in March and October. (Call ahead for the exact dates.) Animals auctioned include various exotic breeds of chickens and rabbits, but there also are doves, llamas, and occasionally longhorn cattle and boa constrictors. There's a small admission price for the exotic auction, but the twice-monthly horse auctions are free to the public. The Eagle Grove Auction Barn is on State 17 north of Eagle Grove. What's the opening bid for, as Elizabeth calls it, a belly-pot pig? In addition to processing meat for sale, LeWright's Locker has added a deli at 317 West Broadway. Ryerson's Antiques on State 17 on the south side of town specializes in Victorian lampshades. From Eagle Grove, backtrack to State 3, and take it east to Clarion, county seat of Wright County.

In Clarion's Gazebo Park on the west side of town is the 4-H Schoolhouse Museum. This one-room schoolhouse was the birthplace of the 4-H emblem, the four-leaf clover representing head, heart, hands, and service to others, in the early 1900s. It contains memorabilia of the beginnings of 4-H, including a variety of uniforms. (For more Iowa connections with the beginning of 4-H, see Chapter 10.) Continue east on State 3 to the town square and the Wright County Courthouse. The Main Street Gallery features Iowa artists, including P. Buckley Moss. The White Fox Gift Shop, 108 Central Street, carries antiques and reproductions. From Clarion, continue east on State 3, south on US 69, and east on County C54 to Dows, where you will find an Iowa Welcome Center in a restored historic depot with Iowa crafts for sale and the Dows Mercantile in a century-old building at 124 Ellsworth Street. The mercantile sells Iowa-made jams and jellies, pottery, jewelry, doll furniture, quilt racks, and other gifts and antiques. Head south on US 69 and west on Old Highway 20 to Webster City, county seat of Hamilton County.

Webster City's Bonebright Museum Complex is a nine-acre park on State 17 that contains several restored buildings, including an Illinois Central Depot, 1866 Hamilton County Courthouse, a one-room school, two original pioneer cabins, and a burial mound. In 1850 Wilson Brewer and his family settled about six miles south of what is now Webster City, and he staked out a claim within what are now the city limits. In 1932 Brewer's grandson, Frank Bonebright, and his sister Harriet Bonebright Carmichael gave the city a tract of land that was part of the original Brewer homestead. Another recommended stop is the Kendall Young Library, 1201 Wilson Avenue, where you will find a collection of dolls and Native American artifacts.

Our trip has come almost full circle, starting at a farm bed and breakfast near Stratford and ending less than twenty-five miles away at another farm bed and breakfast west of Webster City. Tom and Shirley Yungclas, fourth-generation farmers in Hamilton County, own and run Centennial Farm Bed and Breakfast, on Old Highway 20 between Webster City and Fort Dodge. Tom was born in the farmhouse the same year his Model A pickup was manufactured. Parts of the original house are incorporated into the contemporary two-story house. The Yunglases encourage their guests to gather eggs for their full, country breakfast. A special bonus—children are welcome.

In the Area

Hook's Point Country Inn (Stratford): 515-838-2781 or 800-383-7062

Glass and Gifts on Shakespeare (Stratford): 800-365-0402

Country Heather (Stratford): 515-838-4444

Lu's Glass Art (Stratford): 515-838-0001

Yesteryear Antiques (Stratford): 515-838-2855

Cloud's Collectibles (Stratford): 515-838-2493

In Good Company (Stratford): 515-838-2750

Gardini's General Store (Lehigh): 515-359-2914

The Blue Willow Tea Room and Bakery (Harcourt): 515-354-5295

Fort Museum and Frontier Village (Fort Dodge): 515-573-4231

Blanden Memorial Art Museum (Fort Dodge): 515-573-2316

Old Harvester Gifts and Antiques (Fort Dodge): 515-955-6260

Make Mine Country (Fort Dodge): 515-573-8075

Humboldt County Mill Farm Museum (east edge of Dakota City): 515-332-5280

West Bend Historical Museum (West Bend): 515-887-4721

Sod House, Schoolhouse, and Museum (West Bend): 515-887-4721

Grotto of the Redemption (West Bend): 515-887-2371

Field's Antiques (Goldfield): 515-825-3655

Goldfield Cheese Mart and Gift Shop (Goldfield):
515-825-3450

Dakota Shop (Goldfield): 515-825-3394

LeWright's Deli (Eagle Grove): 515-448-3300

Ryerson's Antiques (Eagle Grove): 515-448-3079

4-H Schoolhouse Museum (Clarion): 515-532-2256

Main Street Gallery (Clarion): 515-532-2674

White Fox Gift Shop (Clarion): 515-532-2080

Dows Depot Welcome Center (Dows): 515-852-3595

Dows Mercantile (Dows): 515-852-3533 or 852-3595

Bonebright Museum Complex (Webster City): 515-832-1744

Kendall Young Library (Webster City): 515-832-2565

Centennial Farm Bed and Breakfast (Webster City):
515-832-3050

2 ~

Amish, Czech, and Norwegian Ethnic Tour

From Dubuque: Take US 20 west and State 150 north to Hazelton.

From Waterloo: Take US 20 east and State 150 north to Hazelton.

From Oelwein: Take US 20 south to Hazelton.

Highlights: *Amish farms and country stores, world's smallest church, Fort Atkinson, Czech village of Spillville, Antonin Dvorak memorabilia, Bily Brothers Clocks, Norwegian town of Decorah, Vesterheim Norwegian Museum, Broadway–Phelps Park Historic District, Porter House Museum, Montgomery Mansion Bed and Breakfast, the Farm Park, Seed Savers Exchange, the Laura Ingalls Wilder Museum. Allow at least two days for this trip.*

On this trip, visitors can glimpse three different cultures— Amish farm families, the Czech village of Spillville, and the Norwegian town of Decorah. Geographically, we start on the prairie near Oelwein, but limestone bluffs crop up ten miles north around Fayette. The quintessential country road, through Grannis Hollow, between Fayette and Wadena, winds amongst woods, hills, streams, and across an old railroad bridge. Back on the highway, north of West Union, the road pauses before descending into a picturesque valley, and near Decorah, our route cuts through limestone bluffs along the Turkey and Iowa Rivers.

When I was a little girl in the 1950s, I loved to go shopping with my mother in Oelwein, about thirty miles away from our farm. We rarely bought clothes in stores; most often, my mother sewed them. She ordered a few special ones from the mail-order catalogs. Shoes were a different matter; she bought those for me in a real store, Duffy's in Oelwein. For other reasons, Oelwein became even more fascinating for me.

In rural northeast Iowa, I had little exposure to what we now call multiculturalism. One black family ran a melon stand about fifteen miles away. Other ethnic differences usually amounted to little more than knowing that my friends' grandparents came from Norway, while mine hailed from Switzerland and Germany. It was on the streets of Oelwein that I saw people who looked much different from me. First, we saw the horses and black buggies tied up in the parking lot where we left the car. Then we walked through the back door of Woolworth's, past the aisles of towels, utensils, clothes, and toys, past the soda fountain, and through the front door, out to the main street. There on the sidewalks, I saw a few of the Amish people walking in small groups. Bearded men wore dark hats, dark shirts, suspenders, black trousers, and black shoes. Women dressed in dark bonnets and long-sleeved dark dresses down to their ankles. While I wore shorts, a sleeveless top, and sneakers or a puff-sleeved gingham dress and sandals, the Amish children who peeked out from behind their mothers' skirts wore long, dark clothes. The boys wore little hats and the girls dark bonnets, even on the hottest of August days.

I watched them in fascination, imagining daily life in their homes. (There are about 145 Amish families in the Hazelton-Fairbank-Oelwein area.) The Amish didn't use electricity on their farms. Of course they didn't own television sets or radios—no Mickey Mouse, Lassie, or Sky King, I thought. Horses, instead of tractors, pulled their plows. The

Amish girls

children studied in one-room country schools. They drove horse-pulled buggies or wagons instead of automobiles. Now that, I thought, was neat. I recall hearing stories of Amish boys offering motorists to trade a buggy ride for an hour's spin in a car.

Today, the Amish still keep to many of their traditional ways, but they supplement their farm incomes by selling handmade and baked goods to local non-Amish folks and tourists. The Amish are part of a Protestant group that started in Switzerland. They were named for Jacob Ammonn, who led them in breaking away from the Swiss Mennonites in the

1690s because of disagreements over church discipline; they came to North America in 1728. The Amish sect was more strict and shunned excommunicated members. They teach separation from worldly ways, forbidding members from going to war, swearing oaths, or holding public office. Personal simplicity is a way of life. From Hazelton, go north on State 150, west on State 281, and south on County W13.

You are on Amish Boulevard, where the caution signs feature the silhouette of a horse and buggy. Just past a little building that looks like a one-room schoolhouse, turn west on 112th Street. The first stop is the home of Laura Yutzy, who sells handmade quilts. A horse lazily chewed grass in front of a red barn and a white picket fence. My father and I walked around the side of the simple, white farmhouse to the front door. We knocked and a middle-aged woman with grayish white hair and wearing a small white cap answered the door. "Come in," she said with a slight German clip to her words. She stepped back to let us into the small, enclosed porch, which is her shop. A sign on the wall read, "Warning: Quiltpox. Symptoms include continual need for snuggling under a homemade quilt. Patient has deaf expression, sometimes deaf to spouse and kids. Has no taste for electric blanket . . . Treatment: medication is useless, disease is not fatal. Victim should attend as many sales and country stores as possible." She laughed as we read the sign, and leafed through a stack of quilts three feet thick. They are pieced in many designs including the wedding ring, friendship, log cabin, and star of Texas designs. The hand-pieced and hand-stitched coverlets sell for about $850. "The young (Amish) girls have to learn how to quilt, because they go to these quilting bees," she explained. Showing her tiny, even stitching, she said, "I think what makes a quilt is all that nice quilting." She and her daughter also make homemade noodles, jams, and jellies, including peach, apricot, orange, strawberry, cherry, and elderberry flavors. There's even dandelion jelly, zucchini jam, pear jam, and ground-cherry jam.

I bought a jar of ground-cherry jam that brought back memories of picking them and popping them into my mouth while my grandmother gardened. Ground-cherries grow on low, bushy plants similar to tomato plants. The fruit grows inside papery husks the color of brown paper bags. It was delightful to tear open the little round bag and find the marble-sized, sweet yellow "cherries" inside. Continue west on 112th Street.

On the south side of the road is the Neil Hershberger farm where you can buy old farm tools and some antiques. The Hershberger women had several quilts and homemade jams and jellies for sale. A young barefoot woman in a long dark dress and white bonnet came out to greet us. At home on the farms, men, women, and children often are barefoot, and women and girls wear white bonnets instead of the dark ones they use for going into town. Farther west is a sawmill run by Daniel Borntreger, and turning south on Denison Avenue, you pass the farm of Henry A. Mast, a carpenter who builds custom cabinets. Continue south, then turn east on 140th Street.

Levi Nisley owns a farm and general store on 140th Street. "Last year we sold 3,100 pies and 4,200 loaves of bread," he said as he sat behind a low counter covered with loaves of bread. After buying a peach pie and a dozen cinnamon rolls, we walked to our car. A group of children, rosy-cheeked and barefoot, stopped their foot race to look at us. Two little girls giggled, said something in a dialect that I couldn't understand, then scampered to the farmhouse. Continue east and turn south again on Amish Boulevard until you reach 165th Street.

The Sam Nisley family owns the Pine Grove Store where they sell fabrics, dark hats, and the black Red Wing shoes that many Amish people wear. It was here in 1987 that I bought a handmade bentwood rocker and carted it back to Seattle. Every night since our daughter Elizabeth was born, my husband and I have rocked her in that lovely chair. I like to think that, even though we live a much more hectic life than the Amish, the chair helps us to slow down and appreciate the simple pleasures of sitting quietly, reading aloud, and holding a precious child. Turn around and head back north, turning east on 162nd Street. As the road jogs to Furman Avenue and 160th Street, you will arrive at Miller's Country Store, where Ben Miller and his family sell a few crafts, honey, bulk foods, and some baked goods.

From this tour of the Amish farm stores, you will have seen a lifestyle that is plain and simple, probably more in keeping with what most pioneers experienced than what we see in fancy boutiques advertising the "country look." Take Grant Avenue north and then go west on 120th Street back to Amish Boulevard for the return to State 150 into Oelwein. Head east on State 3 and north on County W33, then east on State 187 to Arlington.

A Queen Anne–style Victorian home on Depot Street is House of Hats, which includes an impressive collection of more than 5,000 hats, including an Amish baby bonnet and head wear from the 1800s. The Quilted Keepsakes and Unique Dolls Museum, one story of a private home at 577 Main Street, features a collection of handmade quilts, premium dolls, and advertising memorabilia. The owner, Mary Jane Lamphier, has written books on quilting, including *Patchwork Plus* and *The Pieceable Kingdom,* but phone ahead, because if she's writing another book, the shop may be closed. The Federal Aviation Airways Facilities Sector Field Office, Iowa's only radar station, is a worthwhile stop. Visitors can learn about air surveillance. Stop at Brush Creek Canyon State Preserve, a 216-acre wilderness with rock chimneys, canyons, and good trout fishing. Continue north on County W51 to Wadena.

For a wonderfully scenic rural drive—and some trout fishing or canoeing, too—head through Wadena and take a left on West Harriman, a T-intersection; this changes to Derby Road, a gravel road, at the city limits. Gravel roads wind through the woods, over hills, across an old railroad bridge, through Grannis Hollow and into Fayette. Continue one mile and take a left on 157th Street. Continue 1.5 miles and take a left on Fox Road, which has a nice trout stream alonside iit. You will cross over a bridge that was once a railroad bridge for the train that ran between Wadena and Fayette. After crossing the bridge you will see a sign on the left for Grannis Creek access road, which is flanked with a profusion of wild ferns. Continue on Fox Road and then take a left onto Grain Road and a right onto Hemlock Road. You will pass a small park with a sign, Langerman's Ford river access, where you can put in your canoe. Take a right onto Kornhill Road. This will bring you into Fayette on Union Street past the new Upper Iowa University athletic field.

Fayette is home of Upper Iowa University. With an enrollment of about 2,800, UIU is the second largest private college in the state, behind Drake University in Des Moines. While on the campus, you can whet your appetite for things to come (ahead in this chapter in Decorah) by looking at the Porter Butterfly Collection with some 1,000 of the insects mounted in cases in the hall of Baker-Hebron Hall. From Fayette take State 150 north.

Follow the signs to the Volga River State Park, the largest recreation area in Iowa, with fishing, boating, camping, bridle trails, hiking, and cross-country skiing and snowmobile trails in winter. Continue on State 150 to West Union, the Fayette County seat. On the courthouse square is the Fayette County Historical Museum with exhibits on local history, war memorabilia, agriculture, and genealogy.

Just a few miles north of West Union on State 150 at the top of a hill is Goeken Park, a perfect vantage point from which to look down into the Turkey River Valley and the town of Eldorado (el-doe-RAY-doe). The view of this village with its towering church steeple set against the surrounding valley is inspiring.

Stop in at the little Eldorado Store for some tasty sausages and bologna. Mike Woodson also sells woven rag rugs and hand-beaded jewelry. Woodson learned to weave in a college fine arts class, and after living in the Dakotas, he became very involved in Indian culture, weaving, beading, and dancing. After moving back to Iowa, he continued to weave and bead. Talking about the plight of small town merchants, Woodson explained, "It used to be that people did all their shopping here. A barber even came in on Wednesday nights and cut hair for the people in the town." The traveling barber and loyalty from local residents have gone by the wayside. "People in this area take this store for granted," he said. "There are a couple of older couples who shop here exclusively, but most of the others will drive miles and miles to a bigger store." From Eldorado, continue north on State 150.

Festina is home to what is believed to be the world's smallest church. A two-mile jaunt west on County B32 takes you to Anthony of Padua Chapel. A log chapel was built on the site in 1849. In 1886 builders used locally quarried stone to construct the current chapel, which seats eight in the four small pews. The chapel grew out of a mother's pledge: if her son were returned safely from the Napoleonic War, she would have a chapel built. He did and she did. From the chapel, continue west on County B32 to Fort Atkinson.

Iowa's frontier days come to life at the Fort Atkinson State Preserve, with the fort partially restored to its 1840 appearance. This fort holds the distinction of reportedly having been built to protect the Winnebago tribe from other native groups, but it paved the way for white settlers. In 1848 the tribe was relocated in Minnesota, and the fort was abandoned in 1849. The historical museum in the old barracks presents a glimpse of daily life at the time. The Fort Atkinson Rendezvous, held the last full weekend of September, recreates frontier life and fur trading activities. From Fort Atkinson, you can continue northeast on State 24, then on Lake Meyer Road, to reach the Lake Meyer Nature Center, which includes a thirty-eight-acre lake, wildlife exhibits, Indian artifacts, and nature trails. Otherwise, head north on County W14 to Spillville.

Visitors find the ambiance of a European village in Spillville, a Czechoslovakian settlement with the old Spillville Mill, St. Wenceslaus Catholic Church, and its cemetery. The town square features a bandstand built at the end of World War I for American soldiers. Riverside Park, a large shady stretch along the Turkey River, commemorates the town's musical tradition with the Inwood Ballroom, where many Big Bands played, and a memorial to Antonin Dvorak.

After a year directing the New York Conservatory of Music, Czech composer Antonin Dvorak and his family chose to spend the summer of 1893 in Spillville. He composed, made corrections on his *New World Symphony*, found inspiration for "Humoresque," and played the organ daily for mass at the 1860 St. Wenceslaus Church. In 1929 a fifty-mile stretch of road was dedicated to the distinguished visitor, who traveled the route from Calmar to Preston, Minnesota, to visit Czech families. The Dvorak Highway goes north from Calmar on US 52, west on State 325 to Spillville, west on County B16 to Protivin, north on County V58 through Cresco to the Minnesota border, passing two historic sites—the house in Spillville where the Dvorak family lived and the church in which he played the organ. The Dvorak Festival is the first weekend in August.

Spillville is well known for Bily Brothers Clocks. Two brother farmers, Spillville natives, hand-carved each of the clocks, starting during the long Iowa winters. The collection is housed in the 1893 summer home of Antonin Dvorak. On the second story, you can see Dvorak memorabilia.

If Czech specialties attract your tastebuds, be sure to dine at The Old World Inn, where standard fare also is available. The day I stopped, smells of sauerkraut and dill wafted through the air. Try the *veprova pecene se zelim* and *houskove knedilky* (roast pork with sauerkraut and bread dumpling with gravy) or the Czech goulash. Weekend all-you-can-eat buffets do not include Czech entrees, but at $5.95, who's complaining? The inn was built in 1871 as a general store, and it later served as a pool hall, butcher shop, and warehouse. Four guest rooms on the second floor feature high ceilings and plenty of windows for an airy ambiance. They are decorated with attractive wallpapers and a mix of traditional and old (though not necessarily antique) furnishings.

Across the street is Taylor Made Bed and Breakfast, in a century-old home owned by the Taylors: Howard, who is Czech, and Clarabelle, who is German. The establishment is decorated with furniture the couple stripped and refinished and handmade rugs, curtains, and linens. Clarabelle bakes fresh bread and/or pastries, including *kolaches,* popular among the Czechs. "Sometimes, I serve *jeternice,* that's a Czech pork sausage," she said. "Even people who have never had it before really like it." From Spillville take State 325 east and head south on US 52 into Calmar to the Calmar Guesthouse. Don't be deceived by the rather plain exterior of this white 1890 Queen Anne–style home. The inside features beautifully refinished woodwork, antiques in every room, and a scrumptious breakfast with homemade quickbreads and muffins. From Calmar head north on US 52 to Decorah. The highway runs parallel to part of the Upper Iowa River, the only stream in the state classified as wild and scenic. The river is popular for canoeing, inner tubing, and bass fishing. There are landing points and canoe rentals at Kendallville, Bluffton, and Decorah.

Whenever I think of Decorah, I think of Nordic Fest, a celebration of Scandinavian traditions, arts, and folkways the last full weekend in July. The last time my parents and I went,

A trunk decorated in Norwegian rosemaling

we watched Norwegian women in traditional costumes milk goats and make cheese. Others turned out mouth-watering delicacies, such as *Kransekake*, Norwegian wedding cake, and *lefse*, an unleavened potato bread that looks like a tortilla and usually is eaten with butter and sugar. Artists demonstrated *rosemaling*, the stylized Norwegian folk painting, and wood carving. Oneota Weavers Guild members used a two-harness loom built in 1898 to weave traditional Norwegian tapestries. The Nordic Dancers, costumed schoolchildren, performed Norwegian folk dances. There are parades, arts and crafts shows, dances, special performances at Luther College, and guests from Norway. In short, visually and gastronomically, it's a festival that will have you saying, "Yah, you betcha' " in no time.

The town of Decorah was named after Waukon-Decorah, a well-known chief of the Winnebago Indians, a peaceful tribe that made their home in the area. The first white settlers came from England in 1849, but immigrants from Norway made this the first Norwegian settlement west of the Mississippi. Glaciers receded before they ravaged the land around Decorah, so the landscape is full of wooded hills and bluffs. The town has been the Winneshiek County seat since 1851, when it flourished with many grain mills. The site of several early grain mills is now Dunning's Spring, a city park, with a waterfall, picnic area, and hiking trails. Today, Winneshiek County is the largest dairy production county in the state. Farming and light industrial manufacturing, as well as Luther College, keep the city of about 8,500 and surrounding area economically healthy.

Downtown, Water and Main Streets are lined with healthy businesses. For those interested in homemade whole wheat cinnamon nut rolls, stroll up the street to Cafe Deluxe. Its other offerings include soups, omelets, steaks, stir fries, pasta dishes, pizzas, and desserts fresh from their bakery. Farther up Water Street is The Window, a large shop with antiques and collectibles.

Don't despair if you happen to miss Nordic Fest. You can learn about Decorah's Norwegian heritage at the Vesterheim Norwegian-American Museum, 502 West Water Street, the country's oldest and largest museum focusing on one ethnic group of immigrants. In the complex that occupies almost an entire city block, you will see elegantly carved furniture, traditional costumes, elaborate fabric, and painted wood decorations, as well as everyday objects in the fourteen historic buildings showing the immigrants' transition from Norway to life in their "western home" in America. The exhibit includes a ship that actually sailed across the Atlantic. The gift shop features Norwegian tapes, music, Christmas music, painted wooden items, jewelry, cards, books, wooden items for crafts, carving tools, gourmet foods, and cards. The Dayton House, next door, features Norwegian entrees and desserts.

Just south of there is the Broadway–Phelps Park Historic District, with examples of nearly all major architectural movements dating back to 1850. The self-guided walking tour (free maps are available at the Decorah Area Chamber of Commerce) includes a home used in the Underground Railroad. Phelps Park overlooks the upper Iowa River.

The Porter House Museum, 401 West Broadway Street, resembling an Italian Tuscan villa, is considered to be one of the finest and best preserved Victorian homes in northeast Iowa. It was built in 1867 of native brick with decorative white trim. The ornate rock wall around it was built by the owner and his helpers from 1939 to 1945. Decorah native Adelbert Field Porter devoted his life to being a collector and naturalist. His three major collections displayed in the mansion include butterflies, moths, and insects; stamps; and rocks and minerals. He also created scenic pictures, jewelry, and trays from butterflies, shells, and flowers. The mansion includes several pieces of Victorian furniture used by English settlers in early Decorah.

About six blocks farther south is the Montgomery Mansion Bed and Breakfast, a restored 1877 Victorian home, featuring period decor and furnishings. A complete breakfast is served in the mansion's grand dining room. If you are looking for a good dinner spot, try the Cliff House, a local favorite, at the junction of US 52 and State 9.

Take College Drive from the west end of Water Street northwest out of town and you will come to Luther College, which moved to Decorah in 1861 from LaCrosse, Wisconsin. The campus, with wooded, rolling hills and several buildings listed on the National Historic Register, is especially picturesque in the fall. Here you can see productions of theater, ballet, opera, and symphony.

Just across from Luther College is a big red barn with a limestone foundation, built in 1868. It is the home of the Farm Park, showplace of the Institute for Agricultural Biodiversity, directed by Hans Peter Jorgensen and Shan Thomas. The couple hired Amish farmers to renovate the barn in their quest to preserve rare breeds of animals that came to the U.S. during the nineteenth century. The barn is named for Andersen Ashmore and Jacob Jewell, two settlers who each built part of the barn in the 1800s. The Farm Park is a museum, zoo, school, and showplace. The couple plans for a "Hall of History" displaying artifacts found in the barn, and a "Hall of Genetics" depicting the significance of biodiversity. "These are live artifacts, as well as spare parts for twenty-first-century genetics," said Jorgensen.

If today's breeds were knocked out by epidemic, the couple fears that the fewer number of farm breeds could be doomed, with no resistant genes to fight disease. The farm features a Norwegian fjord horse, belted Galloway beef cattle, Navajo-Churro sheep, and Jacob sheep. Jorgensen likes to paraphrase Aldo Leopold, well-known conservationist, by saying, "The first precaution of intelligent tinkering is to save all the parts." Until 1967, the 320-acre farm produced food for Luther College. Then the land was rented, and the buildings went into a period of decline before Jorgensen and Thomas rescued them.

Side trip: To reach one of Iowa's oldest school buildings, head northeast out of Decorah on County W38. The Locust School is at the junction of County W38 and County A26. This limestone structure on the National Register of Historic Places was a rural school for 106 years.

Side trip: If you are interested in fishing, travel east on State 9 and watch for signs for the Siewer Springs State Trout Rearing Station, off Trout Run Road, where the state has been rearing trout for stocking rivers and creeks since 1933. Tours are available. Return to State 9 and head southeast on County W4B past Frankville to Sugarbush Farms. Also on State 9 is the Freeport Bowstring Arch Bridge, built in 1879. One of four bridges of this style in the country, it is 156 feet long. Sugarbush Farms, between Castalia and Frankville, has been in the Green family since about 1880. Tree tapping begins in March, with hundreds of gallons of sap boiled down into maple sugar and syrup. Visitors during that time can see the collection and manufacturing methods used. Continue south to US 52 and at Ossian, you can loop back into Decorah on County W42, passing the Washington Prairie Church.

The area's first genetic preservation project, started in 1975, lies north of Decorah. Take US 52 northwest out of town and turn north on County W34 to reach Heritage Farm, which looks like it was plucked off the cover of *Successful Farming*. A white farmhouse and robust red barn (reroofed by Amish carpenters) are flanked by row upon row of healthy green vegetables. This is a 140-acre living museum with an orchard and 8,000 rare garden vegetables. Kent and Diane Whealy started Seed Savers Exchange to preserve seeds of rare vegetables, fruits, and grains after Diane's grandfather, Baptist Ott, gave the couple three jars of morning glory, tomato, and bean seeds that his forebears brought to this country from Bavaria. The couple realized that in order for these varieties to survive, they would have to grow them and harvest the seed. As a result, they became very interested in genetics and the nonhybrid plant varieties being dropped by commercial seed growers. Soon, they ran classified ads in garden magazines for exchanging seeds. Today, they maintain more than 8,000 varieties of rare vegetables and store seeds for exchange among 6,000 members nationwide. The farm also includes an historic orchard of old-time apples, grapes, and horseradish varieties. Seed Savers publishes several books and catalogs, including a 300-page yearbook with names of people wanting to swap plant seeds. Visitors are welcome June through September. Backtrack to US 52 and continue north. Turn right on 236th Avenue into Burr Oak for the Laura Ingalls Wilder Park and Museum.

The books written by Laura Ingalls Wilder, telling of a little girl's pioneer life with her family, have entertained children and adults for years. Laura lived in Burr Oak for about eighteen months. Although there is not much to the town these days, it once thrived as a stopover for more than 200 covered wagons a day on their way to settle the West. In the fall of 1876 after hordes of grasshoppers devastated the crops in Minnesota, Charles Ingalls moved his family to Burr Oak to manage the Master's Hotel, owned by family friend William Steadman. Laura was nine years old. The family moved out of the hotel into their own home in Burr Oak. The time comes between her books entitled *On the Banks of Plum Creek* and *By the Shores of Silver Lake*. In time, Ingalls moved his family back to Walnut Grove, Minnesota.

A pair of hand-carved ivory birds that belonged to Laura are among the hotel/museum's prized possessions. The hotel had a room for the women, one for the men, a stagecoach master's bed at the top of the stairway, and a family room for traveling guests. The Ingalls's room in the basement was so small that one of the children had to sleep on a pallet in the doorway. My guide picked up a corner of the straw tick on the bed to show the rope "springs" beneath it. Burr Oak celebrates Laura Ingalls Wilder Days the first weekend in June.

In the Area

House of Hats (Arlington): 319-633-5855

Quilted Keepsakes and Unique Dolls Museum (Arlington):
319-633-5885

Upper Iowa University (Fayette): 319-425-5200

Fayette County Historical Center (West Union): 319-422-5797

Fort Atkinson State Preserve (Fort Atkinson): 319-425-4161

Lake Meyer Nature Center (Fort Atkinson): 319-534-7145

Bily Brothers Clocks (Spillville): 319-562-3569 or 562-3798

Old World Inn (Spillville): 319-562-3739 or 562-3186

Taylor Made Bed and Breakfast (Spillville): 319-562-3958

Calmar Guesthouse (Calmar): 319-562-3851

Winneshiek County Tourism (Decorah): 319-382-3990

Decorah Area Chamber of Commerce (Decorah):
    319-382-3990

Farm Park, Institute for Agricultural Biodiversity (Decorah):
    319-387-2150 or 387-1865

Vesterheim Norwegian-American Museum (Decorah):
    319-382-9681

Cafe Deluxe (Decorah): 319-382-5589

Cliff House Inn (Decorah): 319-382-4241 or 800-632-5980

Dayton House Norwegian Cafe (Decorah): 319-382-9681

Luther College (Decorah): 319-387-2000

Montgomery Mansion Bed and Breakfast (Decorah):
    319-382-5088

Locust School (Decorah): 319-382-4321

Siewer Springs State Trout Rearing Station (Decorah):
    319-382-8324

The Window (Decorah): 319-382-5773

Heritage Farm, Seed Savers (Decorah): 319-382-5990

Laura Ingalls Wilder Museum (Burr Oak): 319-735-5916

Porter House Museum (Decorah): 319-382-1867

3 ~

The Great River Road— McGregor and North

From Dubuque: Follow US 52 north to McGregor.

From Waterloo: Follow US 20 east, State 13 north, and State 18 east to McGregor.

Highlights: *View of Mississippi from Pikes Peak State Park, old river towns of McGregor and Marquette, Effigy Mounds National Monument, Villa Louis, Froelich Historic Site, Spook Cave. Allow at least two days for the entire trip.*

This route starts at McGregor and follows the Great River Road along the Mississippi River north to Lansing. This scenic drive affords spectacular views of the mighty river, the barges, and towboats that travel this big highway. From high atop the bluffs, you can see eagles and turkey vultures soaring. One of the most interesting facets of this trip is a visit to the effigy mounds, ancient Indian burial sites made in the shapes of birds and bears. Our circular route winds inland through fields of corn, oats, and hay, past barns and country churches, and ends almost 100 feet below the Earth's surface—in a fascinating limestone cave.

A turkey vulture glides overhead; its large wings catch an updraft and send it soaring above the treetops. From a wooded bluff at Pikes Peak State Park 500 feet above the river, my mother, daughter Elizabeth, and I gaze out across the Mighty Mississippi. A powerful little tug pushes a barge, perhaps half a football field in length, upstream. Two houseboats drift lazily, while a water skier deftly jumps the wake left by the barge. Farther to the east, eddies, sloughs, and lakes form the backwaters of this magnificent highway of water. We read the interpretive signs about birds and woodland creatures to Elizabeth. As we walk to a picnic table and prepare to delve into a picnic lunch, a chickadee flits past us. Afterward, Grandma indulges Elizabeth at the playground while I explore the trails and lookouts. Violets, columbine, and milkweed are part of the dense, green underbrush. Other inhabitants are river otters, bald eagles, bluebirds, mallow, jack-in-the-pulpit, lady's slipper, and calypso orchids.

Pikes Peak State Park, two miles southeast of McGregor on State 340, includes 960 acres of timbered land and thirteen miles of foot trails that run from the southern part of the park to McGregor at the north. I have visited this park a half-dozen times but never appreciated it as much as the day I shared it with my mother and daughter. Over the years, park facilities have vastly improved. A large observation deck, handicap-accessible boardwalks, and a children's playground are some of the facilities that make the park enjoyable for many ages and abilities. An Indian burial mound in the shape of a bear is just north of the parking lot and picnic area. From the overlook, visitors can see as far as Prairie du Chien, Wisconsin, which started as a trading center. Slightly southeast is the mouth of the Wisconsin River as it empties into the Mississippi. South and east is Wisconsin's Wyalusing State Park, a 2,600-acre park. *Wyalusing* is a native word meaning "home of the warrior." Backtrack into McGregor.

A ferryboat landing built by Alexander MacGregor and Thomas Burnett in 1837 spawned the settlement of McGregor, which grew into one of the most important shipping depots west of Chicago. When the town was incorporated in 1857, MacGregor (the man) gave permission to drop the "a" from the town's name, and it was called McGregor. By the 1860s, the town had a population of 5,500 and 126 businesses, including twenty that stored or shipped grain and thirty saloons. The pearl industry played an important part in the town's growth. Even those who didn't find pearls in the mussel beds could make money selling the shells to button factories in McGregor, Prairie du Chien, Dubuque, Clinton, and Davenport.

In autumn, the gold, rust, and crimson colors of the leaves are a rich background for the historic buildings downtown. Several are antique shops. One shop on Main Street still carries the words, "Christian Bloedel, wagonmaker" on its front. Visit the Stone Balloon Book Store, a favorite of mine, with a small, private tea garden out back in the summer. The bookstore offers a good selection of books on the Mississippi and the region, and the fresh-baked pastries are scrumptious. Triangle Park, a memorial to the son of one of the town's leading business people, is across the street. Diamond Jo Reynolds, an entrepreneur in the steamboat business, had the park built in honor of his son, who died at age thirty. It is said that later, at his wife's request, he dug down to an artesian well to make a fountain that spouted water twenty feet into the air. The son of Quaker parents, Diamond Joe, it is said, maintained his abstinence from drinking and swearing even in the company of rough river men. Across from the little park, he built a large brick building, still standing, for his living quarters and steamboat office. The Diamond Jo Building was later a billiard parlor and a post office. The building's exterior features intricate sunflower tiles and terra cotta friezes. A shrewd businessman, Diamond Joe's estate was estimated at $700,000 when he died in 1891.

One of McGregor's claims in the halls of history is that it was the starting point for the Ringling Brothers Circus. In 1848, harnessmaker August Ringling moved to America from Europe. He came to McGregor in 1860 with his wife and three sons. When the Dan Rice Great Paris Pavilion Circus came to town, Ringling was asked to repair some leather used by the cannon ball juggler. When Ringling refused to accept payment for his work, he and his family were given free tickets to the circus. Sons Al and Gus were so impressed with the acts that they began staging their own shows in the family backyard. Al became known for balancing a plow on his chin. The brothers, Al, Gus, and John, went on to start the Ringling Brothers Circus.

The McGregor Historical Museum offers several glimpses into the past, including re-creations of a rural schoolhouse, typical kitchen and parlor, war memorabilia and history of the Ringling family, Native American handicrafts, and some examples of Andrew Clemens's sand paintings. A childhood illness left the boy deaf at age five. During summers when he was home from school, he used grains of colored sand found in the area and meticulously placed them in glass containers to make designs and elaborate pictures, even inscriptions.

The twenty-room mansion built by businessman William Huntting, a grain merchant, is one of northeast Iowa's finest examples of Queen Anne architecture. Although you can't tour the interior, the three-story private home overlooking McGregor features nine fireplaces, stenciled walls, parquet floors, bay windows, and a tower.

The River's Edge Bed and Breakfast, a two-story clapboard home located at the north end of the town's Main Street, offers three guest rooms decorated in regional antiques and a front deck overlooking the river. Little Switzerland Inn

Bed and Breakfast on Main Street just up from the bookstore is comfortable and convenient. While you are in McGregor, take in lunch or dinner at the White Springs Tavern and Supper Club, a popular eating spot. In spring and summer, stop by Pocket Seed Perennials, a local nursery, for flowers and garden plants. In the fall, roadside stands abound with crafts and produce for sale.

Side trip: Cross the Mississippi into Prairie du Chien, Wisconsin. On Feriole Island, you can visit the Villa Louis, a cream-colored brick Victorian mansion of the Dousman family displaying an excellent collection of Victoriana. Also at the site are the Museum of Prairie du Chien and the Fur Trade Museum, illustrating development in the western part of the state from a fur trading post to a major transportation center. Hercules Dousman started in business here as an agent for the American Fur Company in 1826. He became wealthy from fur trading as well as from his successful business dealings in railroads and steamboats. In 1870, after his death, his widow and son had the villa built, and the Dousman family lived there into the twentieth century. The only battle of the War of 1812 in Wisconsin was fought on the grounds of the present Villa Louis. From Prairie du Chien, backtrack to US 52 and head north.

On the way toward Marquette, you drive north along the river, past cabins, trailers, and small marinas. The district office for the Upper Mississippi Fish and Wildlife Refuge is on the left. Established in 1924, it extends 261 miles from Wabash, Minnesota, to Cordova, Illinois. This area is unique in that its boundaries are the longest of any wildlife conservation area in the lower forty-eight states. This 200,000-acre region includes eleven dams and locks, creating a maze of sloughs, lakes, and islands, home to more than 290 bird species, 57 kinds of mammals, 45 reptiles and amphibian species, more than 115 kinds of fish, and 540 types of vegetation. Thousands of tundra swans and canvasback ducks use the area during their migrations. There is not much to see at the district office, except for some interpretive signage that informs visitors of some of the conservation successes, such as the fact that the bald eagle and great blue heron, at one time endangered, are now seen quite often. Continue north to Marquette.

Initially called North McGregor, Marquette started in 1857 as a supply station for a railroad that would run through the valley. It became a bustling little community, and a year later boasted a population of 300. In the 1860s the first all-rail route from Chicago to Minneapolis–St. Paul went through North McGregor. The town and railroad suffered severe damage from floods in 1896 and 1916, but both were quickly rebuilt. In 1920 the town was named Marquette for the priest, Jacques Marquette, who, with Father Louis Joliet, were the first white men to explore the upper Mississippi in 1673 and to set foot on Iowa soil.

Once in Marquette, turn west onto North Street to go to the Schoolhouse Mall, 1,500 square feet of space filled with Depression glass, furniture, quilts, and other antiques. My mother and I found a set of green Depression glass dessert plates for my sister, and Elizabeth, who enjoys my flower gardens, discovered a delicate blue and clear glass vase for her own roses. Up the hill behind the school is a church that also has been converted into an antique shop. Backtrack to the highway and continue on State 76 north along the river for three miles to Effigy Mounds National Monument.

Iowa's only national monument, Effigy Mounds, designated by President Harry Truman in 1949, encompasses nearly 1,500 acres and preserves some 191 Native American burial mounds, twenty-nine of which are formed in the effigies of bears and birds. The others are conical and linear-shaped mounds. Burial mounds in the shapes of animals have been found only in this area of Iowa, southeastern Minnesota, southwestern Wisconsin, and northwestern Illinois. At one time, more than 10,000 mounds were in northeastern Iowa alone. Mounds in the park have been dated from 500 B.C. to A.D. 1300. The Great Bear Mound is 70 feet across the shoulders and forelegs, 137 feet long, and 3.5 feet high. The visitor center features a film presentation on the mound builders, a small museum explaining the mounds and displaying some artifacts found there, and gift shop. Guided and self-guided tours are offered along the eleven miles of hiking trails.

Some nine miles north of the monument, just west of State 76, is the Yellow River State Forest encompassing 6,548 acres of timbered hills and valleys ribboned with fast-running trout streams and trails. The area is perfect for rustic recreation, including horseback riding, hiking, primitive camping, and snowmobiling, and groomed trails are available for all levels of cross-country skiing. The river was named by French explorers in the early 1770s. This area was the site of the first sawmill west of the Mississippi; it was built by Capt. Jefferson Davis in 1829. In the late 1800s there were so many mills in the area, it was known as an "industrial valley."

At the junction of State 76 and State 364, the Waukon junction, you will find plenty of fresh seafood at Monk Fish Market. This also is the site of a former processing plant for iron ore mined at Waukon. Parts of the plant can still be seen on the side of the hill. Continue north on State 364. Just north of the junction is Paint Rock Bluff, a sacred limestone wall upon which natives painted animal figures. The bluff was surveyed in 1832 by Daniel Boone's son, Capt. Nathaniel Boone. It also was a navigational aide for riverboat pilots.

The next town north on State 364 is Harpers Ferry. The sand prairie around this area was the site of a large Indian settlement and burial area. You can step back in time if you plan to stay at the 1860 Log House. Built by early settlers, the rustic house features hand-hewn, square oak logs with dovetail ends and original open rafters. It is furnished with a few original pieces from the house, a clawfoot bathtub, and iron beds. To get there, continue north one-half mile on County X52, turn left on Whippoorwill Hollow Drive. The Log House is two miles ahead on the right. Backtrack to State 364 and continue north.

(Lock and Dam No. 9 is near Harpers Ferry, across the river in Lynxville, Wisconsin. It features a viewing platform for watching pleasure boats and the huge barges. To get there, you must cross the river at McGregor or Lansing; each are about equal distance from Harpers Ferry.)

Sandstone bluffs overlook the historic river town of Lansing. The grain bins in the old G. Kerndt and Brothers grain elevator have been opened up to feature local crafts, antiques, and gifts. The Lansing Stone School on Center Street, said to be the oldest school in continuous use west of the Mississippi, was built in 1864 in the Greek Revival style. The cantilevered Blackhawk Bridge, named for the chief of the Sauk and Fox tribes, links Iowa and Wisconsin over a three-mile-long stretch of river and backwaters. For a real river experience, take a backwater cruise aboard the *Sand Cove Queen*, a locally built, forty-nine-passenger Coast Guard—approved paddle wheeler, to see beaver, blue heron, and mallard ducks.

For another great view of the river from a 450-foot overlook, drive up Mount Hosmer with its entrance off of Sixth Street. Visitors can view parts of Iowa, Wisconsin, and Minnesota, and enjoy picnic and playground facilities in this twenty-five-acre city park. The park provides a lovely background for the tall-spired, elegant brick Immaculate Conception Church. From Lansing, head west on State 9.

Side trip: From Lansing, you can continue north on State 26 past the Fish Farm Mounds to New Albin and the Minnesota border. Fish Farm Mounds includes 500 acres of open space around a nucleus of prehistoric Indian mounds. Just north of the mounds, Black Hawk Bluff overlooks the mouth of the upper Iowa River. The bluff and 300 acres are public land for picnicking and hiking. The bluff was the site of the Battle of Bad Ax, which ended the Black Hawk War in 1832. Sauk Indians, trying to escape the major battle on the Wisconsin shore, were attacked by Chief Wabasha's warriors at the base of the bluff. Just a bit north of Fish Farm Mounds is Sand Cove, called "Iowa's only desert." This sandy basin is surrounded by wooded hills and goat prairie bluffs, steep hillsides that probably only goats could graze on. These bluffs are covered with native prairie grass and are relatively free of trees. Rural New Albin contains two interesting barns. The Wiemerslage farmstead barn is a log barn built about 1860. The Reburn twelve-sided barn, off State 26, one-half mile west of State 26 on County A11, was built after 1880 and is on the National Register of Historic Places. Backtrack to Lansing and head west on State 9.

Rolling hills with cornfields and cows grazing in pastures stretch out on either side of the highway. Along the way, you will spot the Landmark Inn, a white Federal-style building with a wide front porch and green shutters, on the north. The building, built in the 1850s, has been a brewery, stagecoach inn, post office, store, bar, tea room, and currently is a restaurant/supper club. The original house was built by John Wakefield, said to have grown up and been commissioned by Abraham Lincoln during the Civil War. Colonel Wakefield is believed to have built a gun house behind the inn for his defense after the "Sioux Uprising" in southern Minnesota and northern Iowa.

You will also pass Lourdes Catholic Church, a stunning example of limestone construction with its tall, narrow steeple rising above the farmers' fields.

In Waukon, visit the Allamakee County Historical Center, in Waukon's restored courthouse. Built of native brick in 1861 in the Italianate and Greek Revival styles, it is now on the National Register of Historic Places. It features rooms furnished in turn-of-the-century style. There also is a log cabin on the grounds. Beautiful old churches include the United Church of Christ and St. Patrick's Catholic Church. An interesting private residence is the Barnes octagon house at 22 East Main Street, built in 1865. It sits on twenty feet of bedrock, and the walls were quarried from the site. The Allamakee Bed and Breakfast is a large, square two-story home on Allamakee Street. The Homestead, one of the largest antique and gift shops in the area, carries Red Wing pottery and quilting supplies.

Just south of town on State 9 and State 76 is Sweeney's House of Clocks, displaying nearly 1,000 antique and handmade clocks, as well as furniture, steam engines, old automobiles, machinery, and tools. The clock collection was started by Ray Tlougan of Spillville when he saved a grandfather clock from a garbage truck. The junk man sold him three other clocks for $5.00, and Tlougan started repairing them. Later, he carved his own clocks with an $18.00 jig saw and a pocket knife. The collection was eventually purchased by Ray Sweeney. The site also includes a four-room log cabin built about 1850 and an early twentieth century kitchen with a wooden ice box and a copper-clad woodburning range. One-quarter mile south of the State 9 and County X12 intersection is the Meier Round Barn. Continue south and then west on State 9 and south on State 51 to Postville.

Postville is home to Dr. John R. Mott, who won the Nobel Peace Prize in 1946. An avid Christian, Mott became national secretary of the YMCA and later secretary of the World Alliance of YMCAs. He traveled the world organizing the World Student Christian Federation. During his life, he worked for

41

unity within and among churches and governments. His boyhood home is one block north of US 52 and US 18, at 255 West Williams Street.

The Millstone Emporium is a large shop attractively filled with antiques, crafts, handmade quilts, gifts, and items for home decorating. The Old Shepherd House, built in 1880, offers four guest rooms and three baths and is furnished with heirlooms and antiques. Guests are pampered with informal afternoon tea, evening snacks, and a full breakfast served in the formal dining room. If you enjoy gardening, take a detour southwest of Postville on State 18, to the Perennial Paradise, where Norma Kerr raises and sells perennials and annuals on the farm she and her husband own. Follow State 18 east of Postville to Monona.

The Monona Historical Society maintains a museum, including what is billed as the world's largest collection of hand-carved chains by longtime Monona resident Elmer Marting.

Five miles east of Monona on the north side of US 18 and US 52 is the Froelich (FRAY-lick) Historic Site, an unincorporated village that helped to revolutionize farming. John Froelich is credited with a number of inventions, including the first tractor, the forerunner of the John Deere tractor. A monument commemorates the site of the building where Froelich made the tractor. The town also boasts the Ironclad Store, which got its name from the fireproof metal sheets on the side of the building to keep sparks from railroad steam engines from starting a fire. The restored shop features memorabilia and tractor history photographs. The town's one-room schoolhouse dates back to 1866. It was moved, along with the original furnishings, from its original site to the Froelich Historic Site. The writing on the blackboard is reportedly from 1906. From Froelich, continue east on US 18 and follow the signs to Spook Cave, just six miles west of McGregor.

Early residents were aware of strange noises emanating from a hole at the bottom of a hill along Bloody Run Creek.

Spook Cave

Townspeople who came out to picnic heard strange, eerie sounds from the hole, and they assumed it was haunted. They began calling it Spook Hole and later Spook Cave. In the 1950s Gerald Mielke discovered the cave at the base of a ninety-foot bluff, and dynamited about 600 feet into the hole. "He didn't know how to swim, so he tied an innertube around his waist and crawled another twelve feet into the natural part of the cave," explained our guide and boat captain. Mielke found that splashing water from far inside the cave made the spooky sounds. He opened the cave to the public in 1955. Visitors can take an underground boat trip to view the results of nature's sculpting over the centuries, seeing flowstone, stalactites and stalagmites, and possibly brown or black bats and salamanders. Bring a jacket, the temperature inside the cave remains a constant 47°F. The main room is 110 feet long, 45 feet high, and 90 feet below ground. At 750,000 years old, the cave is relatively young; most are well over a million years old. Visitors also can enjoy camping, picnicking, and swimming on the grounds.

In the Area

Port of McGregor Chamber of Commerce (McGregor): 319-873-2186

Stone Balloon Book Store (McGregor): 319-873-3357

McGregor Historical Museum (McGregor): no phone

River's Edge Bed and Breakfast (McGregor): 319-873-3501

Little Switzerland Inn Bed and Breakfast (McGregor): 319-873-2057

White Springs Tavern and Supper Club (McGregor): 319-873-9642

Spook Cave and Campground (McGregor): 319-873-2144

Villa Louis, Fur Trade Museum, Museum of Prairie du Chein (Prairie du Chein): 608-326-2721

Schoolhouse Mall (Marquette): 319-873-9664

1860 Log House (Harpers Ferry): 319-586-2548

Backwater Cruises (Lansing): 319-538-4497

The Landmark Inn (between Lansing and Waukon): 319-568-3150

Sweeney's House of Clocks (one-half mile south of Waukon): 319-568-4577

Millstone Emporium (Postville): 319-864-3084

Old Shepherd House (Postville): 319-864-3452

Perennial Paradise (Postville): 319-864-3454

Monona Historical Society (Monona): 319-539-2640 or 539-2689

Froelich Historic Site (Froelich): 319-536-2285

John R. Mott Boyhood Home (Postville): no phone

McGregor History Museum (McGregor)

4 ~

Hills and Valleys of Northeast Iowa

From Dubuque: Take US 52 west and north a mile past Garnavillo, head west on State 128 and south on State 13 to Elkader.

From Waterloo: Take US 20 east and State 13 north to Elkader.

Highlights: *Keystone Bridge, Gilbertson Conservation Education Center, Brick City of Clermont, featuring Montauk, Union Sunday School, Motor Mill, Osborne Center, Wilder Museum. This trip could be done in a day, but allow two for a more relaxing time.*

Approaching Elkader from almost any direction, you can see limestone bluffs. The picturesque Clayton county seat sits on both sides of the Turkey River. This trip winds through hills and valleys of northeast Iowa. We drive up the south side of the Turkey to the Kern Hill, which gives a spectacular view of autumn colors. Descending into the valley, we visit Elgin and the "Brick City" of Clermont. On the return part of the loop, we head back to Elkader on the north side of the Turkey River. The route rises to another ridge and scenic overlook. Near Strawberry Point, travelers are back on the prairie.

The Elkader area escaped leveling by glaciers in the last ice age, so its wooded hills, limestone bluffs, and shady riverbanks lend natural beauty to the area. On the northern outskirts of Elkader, off County X16, is the Four Oaks Golf and Country Club, a nine-hole golf course. A big red barn that sits on a wooded knoll has been renovated for the clubhouse. I've golfed here a handful of times with my dad. The first time, I prepared to tee off only to find myself thoroughly puzzled— the clubs were "backwards." I had picked up my dad's left-handed clubs! We traded, but I needed more than the proper clubs to help my score.

A handful of historic sites are at the intersection of High and Bridge Streets, across the bridge from the business district. The stately Clayton County Courthouse was built in 1877 after Elkader was picked as the permanent county seat. It features an 800-pound bell, bought for $190 by the residents of the county, and a clock in the tower, purchased for $550 by the townspeople. On the southeast corner of the intersection is the Greek Revival–style Carter House Museum, with pillars and shutters, built in 1850 by Ernest and Harry Carter. It opened as a museum in 1985 and contains many original furnishings and a collection of rare porcelain and antique china.

The first permanent settlers came in 1836, and the town was laid out in 1845 by three men. One admired Abdel Kader, emir of Algeria who led his people against a French invasion in 1832. Later while in exile in Damascus, the young leader saved 12,000 Christians from an attack by a mob. This early resident suggested the last parts of this leader's name be used to name the new town, hence the name Elkader. Now Elkader and Mascara, Algeria, the home town of Abdel Kader, are sister cities.

From High Street, turn northwest (right) onto Bridge Street and you immediately cross over the Kyestone Bridge, built in 1888 at a cost of $16,000; at 346 feet, it is the longest bridge of its type west of the Mississippi River. The bridge was built in nine months with stone from a local rock quarry.

A great way to enjoy a view of the bridge, the Turkey River, and the courthouse is from the patio of the Keystone Restaurant, Patio, and Saloon. On a summer's evening, it's the perfect place for a drink or dinner. The courthouse bell-tower glistens in the low light, and you may see canoeists paddling down the river. The restaurant building has been an eating establishment for some 140 years, according to owner Keith Knospe, who also has a construction company. His workers renovated the building after a 1990 flood that sent fish into the basement.

On Main Street, the Elkader General Store, 107 North Main Street, is a contemporary version of the old-time model. Visitors can sit at a handful of tables and order simple meals, buy fresh-ground coffee or bulk spices, and even meet with an insurance agent in the back of the room. The Glesne Coast-to-Coast Store, 201 North Main Street, the oldest store in Elkader, is run by the third generation of the Glesne family. There are several antique shops on Main Street. My personal favorite is The Buttery, 118 West Bridge Street, a great shop for antiques, handmade quilts, unique housewares, jewelry, and books.

Catch a production at the Old Elkader Opera House, a three-story, square-front building. In 1903 it took only a month for Elkader residents to buy $10,000 worth of stock to pay for most of the building, replacing the Turner Opera House, which was destroyed by fire in January of that year. The new opera house was built "with a handsome front of pressed brick," as the local newspaper described it. Special trains were run from McGregor and other communities for the opening in November 1903. A 1974 renovation included installation of light fixtures reminiscent of the early 1900s gas lights and a ruby glass chandelier.

One of my most vivid memories of Elkader is St. Joseph's Catholic Church, at First and Boardman Streets, with its towering spire flanked by a blanket of autumn color on the wooded hill behind it. An example of Victorian Gothic architecture, the limestone church was completed in 1898. If you plan an overnight stay, consider the Elkader Bed and Breakfast, owned by Mike and Debbie Wilson. The 1892 Queen Anne mansion features several stained glass windows, hardwood floors, and an ornate oak fireplace.

For a scenic view of the town, drive northwest on Bridge Street and turn right on Second Street S.W., which becomes State 56. Drive up the hill, turn off on one of the side streets, and take in a view that includes Elkader and the Turkey River. In summer, the wooded hills are a glade of green. In autumn, the scene is a riot of leafy color.

Head west on State 56, a ridge that gives great views of hilly farms, red barns, and small dairy herds for about twelve miles. Turn north on County W51 toward Elgin, and in about two miles you will find yourself at the top of the Kern Hill, which in autumn gives motorists a splendid view of dark red oaks, crimson sumac, and golden maples. Travel through the valley to Elgin, pegged as capital of the "Switzerland of Iowa." The hills and small farms are reminiscent of areas of Switzerland, and you will detect several Swiss accents if you talk to many of the locals.

After crossing the bridge over the Turkey River, turn right onto County B64, and in about a mile you will come to the Gilbertson Conservation Education Area, a 327-acre park donated by the late Millard Gilbertson. This and the Osborne Center (see below) rank tops according to my nephews Aaron and Landon and my daughter Elizabeth. Going to see Grandma and Grandpa is synonymous with visiting the 1878 farmhouse and the petting zoo with pygmy goats, bunnies, calves, piglets, and kittens. There's also a Turkey River canoe access, handicapped trail, plots of land showing various types of conservation practices, and a fully operational sawmill built in the 1930s.

Every five years—the next one is in July of 1994—Elgin hosts a homecoming for current and former residents and friends. The festivities include a professionally directed musical production, parade, programs in the city park, and food booths. Continue through Elgin on County W51 to Clermont.

I can't think of Clermont without remembering the taste of homemade *lefse* that my schoolmate Nancy Nelson's grandmother made. Nancy helped by peeling potatoes that were then boiled, mashed, and mixed with flour to make the flat bread. We sat around the Nelson breakfast table eating *lefse* with cinnamon and sugar and a side of deer sausage that Nancy's dad, William, had shot in the fall. I also remember *krube*, a Norwegian blood pudding, that my friend Debbie Aanes said "looks just like chocolate cake," as she dished up a bowlful for herself and poured cream over the top of it for a hearty breakfast. I reached for the cornflakes. The town, predominantly a Norwegian settlement, celebrates Syttende Mai, Norwegian Independence Day, on May 17.

Tourist literature deems Clermont the Brick City. Many of the downtown buildings are made of native bricks. In 1909 alone, more than three million bricks were made. The most well known of Clermont buildings is historic Montauk, the estate of Iowa's twelfth governor, William Larrabee. Imagine my surprise when my tour guide was my cousin Judy Grimm. The mansion, located a mile north of Clermont on North Hill overlooking the Turkey River Valley, was home to the Larrabee family for more than 100 years. The name comes from the lighthouse on Long Island that helped to guide Mrs. Larrabee's father home from whaling missions. Until her death at age ninety-six, Anna, the Larrabee's youngest of seven children, maintained the fourteen-room home as it was when her father was alive. The home is made of brick kilned in Clermont and native limestone. It has been preserved with thousands of books, Wedgwood china, Tiffany lamps, and items from Larrabee's world travels. Also on the forty-six-acre grounds where peacocks and turkeys once roamed, a well house, laundry, creamery, ice house, workshop, and barn have been preserved.

Larrabee was born into a Connecticut seafaring family, but after losing his right eye in a gun accident, he abandoned life as a sailor. Instead he set out for Iowa at the age of twenty-one. He put his intelligence, charm, and persistence to use and by 1857, only four years after arriving, he owned the local grain mill. Four years later, he married Anna Appelman, daughter of a Connecticut sea captain, after she had moved to Iowa. In 1874 Larrabee built Montauk. Larrabee helped found the Republican party in Iowa and served seventeen years in the state senate and two terms as governor. He campaigned to give women the right to vote in local elections as a move toward universal suffrage.

In addition to Montauk, Larrabee left a considerable legacy to the community. In 1896 he had a large pipe organ installed in the Union Sunday School, which was built in 1858 and used by Roman Catholic, Presbyterian, Methodist, and Norwegian Lutheran parishioners. The organ, restored in 1980, is still considered to be the largest Kimball pipe organ in the country. In 1912 Larrabee built his dream school, with a second floor museum encouraging "hands-on" experience with exhibits. The museum was later moved to a bank building on Mill Street.

Mill Street (the main street) features several of the brick buildings, including Burkard Riegel's Blacksmith's Shop, which displays his tools, horseshoes, and information about blacksmithing; the Clermont Opera House, built in 1912, which has been completely restored; and the Clermont

Montauk, the Clermont home of Iowa's twelth governor,
William Larrabee

Museum in the 1913 Clermont State Bank. The museum still carries on Larrabee's vision of focusing on local history. Head east out of Clermont on County B60 three miles past Gunder and watch for a sign for Mary Anne Keppler's Country Calico. Since 1984, Mrs. Keppler has featured an amazing variety of calico fabrics and quilting patterns, as well as classes, in her farmhouse. Take County X16 back to Elkader, then head south on State 13 and County X3C.

What is left of the town of Motor lies five miles southeast of Elkader. The Motor Mill, six-and-one-half stories tall, believed to be the tallest mill in the Midwest, took German stone masons two years to build from 1867 to 1869. The limestone walls are five feet thick at the river level, narrowing to two feet at the top. During its operation, the mill ground animal feed from oats and rye. Buckwheat was ground for pancake flour, and wheat was milled into flour for bread. The town of Motor thrived, and a railroad was started to connect it with McGregor, but an 1875 flood destroyed the construction and the spur was never rebuilt. In 1867, 1871, and 1887, a scourge of chinch bugs and other insects devastated wheat and corn crops, and by 1882, the mill closed. A cooperage, ice house, inn, livery, and a steel bridge are still standing. An effort is underway to research the history of the mill and restore and develop the area. Mill equipment on display was donated from an old mill near St. Ansgar. Canoe access to the Turkey River and two nature trails have been developed on the 100-acre site. Backtrack to State 13.

Four miles south of Elkader on State 13 is the Chicken Ridge Scenic Overlook Park, a vista from which you can see the Turkey and Volga River valleys, and on clear days, you can see all the way to Wisconsin. Continue south another mile to Osborne.

Kids love Osborne Center, the first nature center in the state, started more than thirty years ago. Children love to look at the more than fifty species of Iowa wildlife, although my daughter expressed some dismay, saying, "Mommy, I think they'd be happier outside the cages." The 300-acre center also includes an Iowa Welcome Center; the pioneer village of Osborne; a pond for fishing, sledding, and ice skating; a fitness trail; a nature trail; a land use/conservation trail that demonstrates ecological practices; and hiking/cross-country ski trails. The nature center is really a mini-natural history museum. It includes a touch-and-feel table with furs and hides, live reptile exhibit, geological display, and changing exhibits. The Iowa Room is a gift shop with crafts, gifts, and specialty food items, including books, candles, wooden duck calls, cheese, paintings, caramels, honey, and popcorn, and hand-crocheted, knitted, and quilted items, all made in Iowa. The center is named for Thomas Osborne, who founded the small town of Osborne in 1878 when he subdivided his farm. Residents of the town numbered fifty by the time the railroad arrived. A stagecoach ran between Osborne and Elkader to transport passengers arriving on the train. But when the depot burned, the town started to falter, and by 1935, the railroad was unnecessary. The town that once had a general store, hotel, post office, and blacksmith shop nearly disappeared from sight. The Clayton County Conservation Board put Osborne back on the map, and each year more than 200,000 visitors stop by.

Head west on County C24, a curving road that parallels the Volga River, to reach the town of Volga with its Tractor Land Museum, featuring more than 1,000 tools, tractors, and pieces of farm equipment and the restored Opera House. Continue southwest on State 13, a straight ride across relatively flat farmland, to Strawberry Point.

The town was so named because visiting traders and railway workers enjoyed the plentiful wild strawberries found along local trails. The Wilder Museum is on State 3 across from the post office. Word of the museum's collection of 800 heirloom dolls has left many men, believing that the museum is just a doll museum, sitting in their cars while their wives view the collection; however, those who look will find an extensive arrowhead collection, antique furniture, farm equipment, soapstone carvings, handmade toys, and a children's room with antique toys, games, and apparel. A 1985 addition houses an invaluable collection of porcelain, bisque, china, Victorian glassware, and furniture, the likes of which would qualify for a Sotheby's auction bill. The most popular item in the collection, from the estate of former director Marcey Alderson, is a Victorian table lamp from the movie *Gone with the Wind*.

At Strawberry Point Drug, you can relive a pleasure of the early 1900s, the ice-cream soda, at the store's solid marble bar backed with oak and leaded glass. Go through town and take State 13 and State 3 to County W69 to Devil's Backbone State Park, Iowa's oldest state park, 2.5 miles southwest of Strawberry Point. The 1,750-acre park was named for the high ridge of rock in the center of the park, and it offers unusual rock formations, climbing and rapelling, a large network of hiking trails, swimming, camping, boat rentals, cross-country skiing, and snowmobile trails.

Continue south on County W69, and a mile north of Dundee you'll find the Red Barn Model Railroad Museum featuring displays of Lionel, American Flyer, and Marx toy trains from the early 1900s, three operating Lionel trains, a Lionel trolley, and full-sized railroad memorabilia. Our trip ends here, but you can go west on State 3 to Oelwein and pick up the tour of Amish farms and shops (see Chapter 2).

In the Area

Please phone ahead, as several attractions are open only seasonally.

Keystone Restaurant, Patio, and Saloon (Elkader):
319-245-1992

Elkader General Store (Elkader): 319-245-1799

The Buttery (Elkader): 319-245-1406

Elkader Bed and Breakfast (Elkader): 319-245-1522

Gilbertson Conservation Education Center (Elgin):
    319-426-5740

Montauk (Clermont): 319-423-7173

Union Sunday School (Clermont): 319-423-7173

Clermont Museum (Clermont): 319-423-7173

Mary Keppler's Country Calico (Gunder): 319-426-2445

Osborne Center (Elkader): 319-245-1516

Strawberry Point Information Center (Strawberry Point):
    319-933-4417

Wilder Museum (Strawberry Point): 319-933-4920 or
    933-4472

Devil's Backbone State Park (Strawberry Point): 319-924-2527

Red Barn Model Railroad Museum (Dundee): 319-924-2482

5 ~

The Great River Road— Dyersville, Dubuque, Guttenberg

From Dubuque: Take US 20 west to Dyersville (about twenty-five miles).

From Waterloo: Take US 20 east to Dyersville (about sixty-five miles).

Highlights: Field of Dreams site, *National Farm Toy Museum, Dyer-Botsford House, Basilica of St. Francis Xavier, Heritage House Museum, Guttenberg riverfront, Lock and Dam No. 10, Guttenberg Bible; Cable Car Square, Dubuque Arboretum/Botanical Gardens, Dubuque Museum of Art, Fenelon Place Elevator Company, Mathias Ham House Historic Site,* Spirit of Dubuque, *Woodward Riverboat Museum. Although you could squeeze this trip into a day, it's best to allow at least two.*

It used to be that northeast Iowa meant dairy herds, hills, cornfields, hills, barns, hills, winding roads—and more hills. Now, you can add baseball to the list. After the movie *Field of Dreams,* Dyersville in northeast Iowa has become a sort of shrine dedicated to the love of baseball. Our route starts in Dyersville, meanders cross-country to Dubuque, and then follows the Great River Road through Balltown and north to the German town of Guttenberg, ending up in Garnavillo.

Dyersville, mistaken for heaven in the film *Field of Dreams,* is heaven for many children's fantasies. Not only can

Field of Dreams *farm in Dyersville*

children and their parents visit the ball diamond carved out of a cornfield as depicted in the movie, they can visit a collection of more than 25,000 toys at the National Farm Toy Museum, see more than 900 dolls at the Dyer-Botsford House, visit six toy stores, and see three farm toy manufacturers in Dyersville. My nephew Landon, age four, with two grandpas and several uncles who are or have been farmers, was excited about visiting Dyersville; he knew it started with "T" and ended with "ractors." My daughter Elizabeth, age five, was excited to share the backseat with someone her size. With my sister-in-law, Barbara Wenger, as my copilot, first we stopped at the ballfield.

Field of Dreams has more than one Iowa connection. While at the Iowa Writer's Workshop in Iowa City, writer W. P.

Kinsella wrote a short story that later became the book *Shoeless Joe*. Joe Jackson played on the scandal-ridden Chicago Black Sox baseball team in the early 1900s. In the book, a voice from heaven tells an Iowa farmer (played by Kevin Costner), "If you build it, he will come" and to "ease the pain." Not understanding but believing, the farmer builds a baseball field, and who should emerge from the cornfield dressed to play baseball and build a better relationship with his son but the farmer's father, a fan of Joe Jackson's. Hollywood developed a script, and after looking at sites in a number of states, the producers settled on two farms three miles northeast of Dyersville. With Iowa cornfields in the background, the redemption of father and son, baseball team and fans, took place. Filming took fourteen weeks in the summer of 1988. For the final shot, some 1,000 local cars and trucks were choreographed to come into the ballfield from surrounding country roads.

Like the ghosts of baseball players who emerged from the cornfield to play ball in the movie, visitors started showing up in May 1989. No one was more surprised than Al and Rita Ameskamp, who had plowed under their portion of the ballfield. Don Lansing, owner of the farmhouse in the movie, had left his portion of the field intact. "So many people came to see the field and play on it, even without third base," explained Al, that the Ameskamps reinstated their portion of the field in 1990. That fall, while a Sunday afternoon crowd milled about, Keith Rahe and several semipro baseball players, dressed in vintage uniforms like those in the film, walked out of the cornfield to play ball. Since then, the "Ghost Players," several of whom appeared in the movie, have appeared at the site to entertain visitors and raise money for charity.

The ballfield has become a sort of shrine representing the love of baseball, the pursuit of a dream, and the opportunity many of us fail to take to set things right with a parent or a child. The visitor list has included Reggie Jackson and baseball Hall of Famers Bob Gibson, Lou Brock, and Bob Feller. Several weddings have been held on the premises, and some folks have even requested that their ashes be scattered over the famous ballfield after their death. We sat on the grass and ate a picnic lunch while little sluggers attempted to hit the balls their fathers slow-pitched to them.

But Landon was more interested in tractors than baseball, so we headed for Ertl, a name as dear to him as Barney the dinosaur. Dyersville, one of the state's economically healthiest towns, is home to three farm toy manufacturers, Ertl Toy Company, Scale Models Company, and Spec-Cast. Spec-Cast makes pewter replicas of farm equipment; Scale Models makes die-cast scale models. The Ertl Toy Company offers factory tours, where you can see the manufacturing process from start to finish, but you must make reservations (319-875-2727). Founder Fred Ertl, Sr., a journeyman molder, worked for Dubuque John Deere Works and built his first models in his home with the help of his family, using melted-down surplus aluminum aircraft pistons from World War II. In 1947 the family moved to a small factory in Dubuque and then in 1959 to Dyersville. The company opened its inhouse Farm Toy Museum in 1982.

Today, the National Farm Toy Museum is just northeast of the intersection of State 136 and US 20. It is financed through sales of collector toy tractors produced annually by the Ertl Company. As we walked into the museum entrance, Landon announced, "There's a John Deere." To which Elizabeth replied, "Is it alive?"

The museum features farm toys manufactured from around the world, a full-scale farmhouse verandah, the first Ertl toy ever made, a John Deere riding tractor display, dioramas depicting farms from various decades, and antique farm toys valued at up to $5,000. The museum's video talks about collecting farm toys, as well as the history of and interest in farm toys. Dyersville is home to the Toy Collectors Club of America, and each year the town hosts the Summer Toy Festival early in June and the National Farm Toy Show in the fall. The kids raced from one diorama to the next, with Landon explaining the farm scenes to Elizabeth. "That's the cow, that's the bull, and there's the 'nure loader," he said patiently.

Country nostalgia is the theme of the Toy Farmer Country Store, directly across from the museum, with books, children's toys, and Iowa crafts.

There's nothing like hearty, home-cooked meals to celebrate country living, and you will find exactly that at Country Junction, at the junction of State 136 and US 20. The restaurant is filled with old school desks, farm tools, an Amish wagon, machinery, and gadgets of days gone by. Even the restrooms are reminiscent of farm nostalgia, with hearts and pigs stenciled on the walls, stalls built of weathered wood, and horsecollars framing the mirrors. The barn architecture, designed and built as a tribute to Iowa's farming heritage by Jerry and Jeanine Koch, features huge beams, original silo boards, barn boards, and beveled siding gathered from across the state. The menu features fresh produce, meats, and dairy products, including smoked Iowa pork chops, prime rib, and steaks. Tegeler's ice cream made fresh in Dyersville's own dairy won our group's "Silent Star Award"—we were all too busy eating and enjoying it to talk.

Long before toy tractors or movies drew tourists to Dyersville, the area drew settlers from England and later Germany. Two historic structures in downtown Dyersville, the Dyer-Botsford Historical House and the Xavier Basilica, testify to these roots. The founder of the town, James Dyer, a twenty-seven-year-old from Somersetshire, England, came to farm and to secure property for friends and relatives. He farmed and lived in a log cabin, then he built a fine home on a wooded knoll. Materials for the home were brought by wagon from Dubuque, and it took five years to build it. His friends followed and the settlement of Dyersville was

61

established. Before he died at the age of forty-four, Dyer moved into an eighty-room hotel he was building (which was later destroyed by fire) and sold his home to a mill owner, Abel Botsford of Dubuque, whose family lived in it for 108 years. After it was unoccupied for years, the house was slated for demolition until the Dyersville Area Historical Society bought it in April 1988.

Today, after thousands of hours of work by local volunteers, the three-story house is painted a lemony yellow with bright white trim on the Victorian front porch. Inside, it features authentic Victorian wallpaper, white iron beds, fancy wicker chairs, and a revolving German feather Christmas tree with hundreds of German ornaments. The collection of 900 dolls—including collector dolls of John Wayne, Marilyn Monroe, and Shirley Temple—are set amongst old buggies, tiny china dishes, cradles, and toys. Definitely more toward Elizabeth's tastes than Landon's.

Bavarians arrived in the Dyersville area about 1846. The English community headed by Dyer turned out to be too small and weak to carry out his expansionary vision for the area. The country's Panic of 1857 hurt them further, since many had put their resources into a development program for the town. Many sold their resources to the growing population of frugal German Catholics, and Dyersville became a strong Catholic center.

From 1887 to 1889, after the Catholic congregation outgrew the original church and an expansion, parishioners built St. Francis Xavier, one of only thirty-three minor basilicas in the U.S., at a cost of $100,000. Workers used the block and tackle of rope and pulleys to hoist materials more than 200 feet to the top of each spire. The church contains sixty-four stained glass windows, carved confessionals, frescoes, high vaulted ceilings, the high altar of Italian marble and Mexican onyx, and a large pipe organ. Today, its parishioners outnumber the people of Dyersville. It was proclaimed a minor basilica by

Pope Pius XII in 1956. There are five major basilicas, all in Rome, and Xavier was the twelfth minor basilica, the only one in a rural area, to be dedicated in the U.S.

To rank as a basilica, a church must have been consecrated. The twelve candle brackets and gold-painted crosses at eye level along the interior walls show that this is a consecrated church. In order to be consecrated, a church must be debt free and its main altar must be based on a solid foundation resting on the ground. This basilica is one of the best examples of the true Medieval Gothic architecture found in the Midwest. Xavier's main altar rests on a solid rock foundation.

In the town, signs point the way to the Heritage Trail, a twenty-six-mile-long trail following an old railroad bed across prairies and farmland from Dyersville to Dubuque. The trail features an easy one percent grade for hikers and bicyclists; no horses or motorized vehicles are permitted.

On your way out of town, drive north on State 136. To reach Becker Woodcarving Museum, turn east on Floyd Road and north into Becker Lane. Here, Jack Becker, a native Iowan of Austrian descent, exhibits his talents as a woodcarver with several clocks, a carving of Christ and the twelve Apostles, and other carvings.

State 136 travels north five miles past rolling pastures and cornfields from Dyersville to New Vienna, a small community first settled by five German Catholic families. The town was named for Emperor Francis I of Austria for his support of American Catholic missions.

On the east side of the highway, Kerper's Country Store, a fourth-generation general store, is surrounded by plants in the summer. Jacob Kerper, great-grandfather of the current owner, Steve Kerper, peddled goods between New Vienna and Farley during the Civil War. Kerper still has store invoices dating back to 1870. The current store was built in 1882 of white pine logs floated down the Mississippi from LaCrosse, Wisconsin. Kerper's personal interests are evident in the store—in addition to groceries, meat, and household items, he sells his own hand-carved, hand-painted duck decoys, limited edition art prints, antiques, and hunting supplies.

The beautiful St. Boniface church sits on the west side of the highway. The Gothic-style church built between 1883 and 1887 features a famous Schuelke Tracker Organ made in 1891 and hand-carved altars. The St. Boniface Labor Day picnic is an annual event serving fried chicken and ham dinners and featuring games and dancing. The kids gave up and took naps in the car, while Barb and I took turns visiting the town's museum, which was definitely worth the effort.

Opposite the church is the Heritage House Museum, one of the best small-town museums in the state. More than twenty volunteers have worked to refurbish the former twenty-two-room convent into rooms representative of a late 1800s-era kitchen; summer kitchen with a washboard, tub, and curtain stretcher; dining room; sitting rooms; and bedrooms. The museum features a display of locally made quilts, and local quilters are usually busy working on another one. Other rooms display memorabilia from church, business, the military; school life including uniforms, trophies, and class photos; a nun's room; and farm life including old cream separators, butter churns, and harnesses. At Christmas, volunteers in period dress re-enact activities, such as spinning, baking in the woodstove, and playing the organ. We called it a day, and I made the rest of the trip on another day.

Continue north to Luxemburg, then east on US 52 and State 3 toward Dubuque.

The city of Dubuque was named for Julian Dubuque, a French fur trader who in 1788 was allowed by the Fox Indians to work the lead mines in the area. The first permanent white settler in what is now Iowa, Dubuque was buried with honors befitting a chief. Dubuque is a lovely river city with old brick buildings and brick streets. Here is just a sampler of the many attractions in Dubuque:

- Fenelon Place Elevator Company gives new meaning to the ninety-minute lunch. In the early 1880s it took half an hour to drive the horse and buggy around the bluff to go home for lunch. Ditto for the return trip. J. K. Graves built a private incline railway, so that he could eat his lunch and take a thirty-minute nap and still get back to work. Several fires later, the town still uses the line. The elevator burned in 1884 and Graves rebuilt it; this time he charged neighbors five cents a ride. In 1893 the elevator burned again, but the recession prevented Graves from rebuilding it. Instead ten neighbors formed the Fenelon Place Elevator Company and rebuilt it. By 1916 an apartment was added to the structure where the men met to smoke and play cards away from their wives' scrutiny. Another fire cropped up in 1962, and in 1977 the cable cars were completely rebuilt.

- Cable Car Square is at the base of the Fenelon Place Elevator in the heart of Cathedral Historic District. Here you will find row houses built between 1850 and 1870, St. Raphael's Cathedral built between 1852 and 1859, and a variety of shops and boutiques.

- Dubuque County Courthouse reflects the decoration of the Victorian/Edwardian period. A combination of several architectural elements, it includes Richardsonian-Romanesque and beaux arts classicism. The building is made of limestone, brick, and molded terra cotta and has recently had gold leaf applied to the dome.

- Dubuque County Old Jail/Dubuque Museum of Art, built between 1857 and 1858 of native gray limestone with cast-iron columns and window and door frames, is one of only three in the country designed of Egyptian revivalist architecture, shown by the lotus entry columns and winged lion heads on the window lintels. It was used as a jail until 1971 and is now an art museum.

Dubuque Museum of Art

- The Woodward Riverboat Museum, at the Port of Dubuque's Ice Harbor, explores 300 years of river history through hands-on and life-sized exhibits. In this same complex is the Port of Dubuque Iowa Welcome Center; the National Rivers Hall of Fame, honoring America's greatest river heroes; and the Harbor Place Mall, containing a variety of gift, craft, and antique shops. Visit the sidewheeler *William M. Black,* a 277-foot-long steamboat, open for public tours, or take an excursion cruise aboard the *Spirit of Dubuque,* built in the tradition of the Mississippi paddle wheelers. Trips range from a ninety-minute sight-seeing cruise to a 3.5-hour trip with a prime rib dinner and entertainment on Saturday nights.

- Five Flags Theater, Fourth and Main Streets, was built in 1910, modeled after the Moulin Rouge and Olympia Music Hall in Paris. Dubuque has seen five flags fly over the city— England, Spain, the U.S., and two French flags—hence the name for the theater.

- Mathias Ham House Historic Site, 2241 Lincoln Avenue, an 1856 Italianate villa built of limestone, sits just below Eagle Point Park and has views of the Mississippi River. Owner Mathias Ham, one of the area's first settlers, founded mines and a smelter at Eagle Point in 1833. Costumed guides tell about life at the time and discuss the elegant Victorian furnishings, gilt moldings, and plaster cornices on the thirteen-foot ceilings, all reflecting the splendor of antebellum Dubuque. The site also includes an 1883 one-room schoolhouse and double log house, the oldest building in Iowa.

- Dubuque Arboretum/Botanical Gardens is a living library for garden lovers, from novice to professional. It features a rose garden, prairie grasses, iris garden, bulb garden, perennial garden, waterfall garden, sunken garden, home garden learning center, gift shop, and botanic library.

- Farmer's Market, Thirteenth and Iowa Streets, is an open-air market with fresh, homegrown fruits and vegetables and handmade products, Saturdays until noon, May through November.
- St. Luke's United Methodist Church, 1199 Main Street, is a massive limestone church, Romanesque in style, that features a number of Tiffany stained glass windows. The church was built in 1897.
- Redstone Inn, Fifth and Bluff Streets, is a three-story red brick and stone home built in 1894 by industrialist A. A. Cooper, manufacturer of wagons and buggies, as a wedding present for his daughter, Elizabeth. The opulent parlor features stained glass, cherry-stained oak, and bird's-eye maple. Antique furnishings and Victorian decor are seen throughout the inn.
- The Hancock House, 1105 Grove Terrace, is a three-story Queen Anne house built in 1891 for grocery distributor Charles Hancock. The house features a turret, veranda, and gingerbread trim and an antiques-filled interior with nine guest rooms. Breakfast includes a hot entree, fresh fruit, and homemade pastries.

Head northwest out of Dubuque. At Sageville, proceed northwest on County C9Y toward Sherrill and Balltown.

This winding, hilly road is one of the most scenic drives in the state in autumn. It trails alongside the Mississippi River past the Turkey River Mounds, a native burial site. At times, the road rides a ridge high above farmlands, giving motorists a vantage point similar to that found in Grant Wood paintings. In Balltown, cars were lined up along both sides of the road. Most the occupants were crammed into Breitbach's Country Dining, across from Breitbach's Nutrena Feeds. The restaurant, pegged as Iowa's oldest bar and restaurant, has been in business since 1852. Jacob Breitbach, great-great-grandfather of the current owner, was employed by the original owner and bought the business in 1891. Don't be dismayed by the sort of ramshackle exterior and several additions tacked onto the main house—the restaurant's reputation for great food made from scratch is widespread, and reservations are a must. The establishment is filled with antiques, turn-of-the-century furniture, quilts, and other country crafts. There's even a horse blanket reportedly left by one of the Jesse James gang. After eating (don't forget dessert), proceed to Millville at US 52.

Before reaching Guttenberg, you can take County C7X west, and just east of Garber you will see the Plagman (pronounced PLOW-man) Barn. The barn was built between 1924 and 1925, contracted by Bill Plagman to be of balloon construction, and was used as a dance barn. Admission to the first dance was thirty-six cents. From 1925 through 1939, big bands led by the likes of Duke Ellington and Lawrence Welk played at dances here. Sleeping children lay in a loft on one end while their parents danced. There was a hallway from the entrance directly to the kitchen where people could buy a drink and not pay for dancing. Bootlegging was rumored to have occurred here during Prohibition. Today, the barn and surrounding twenty-seven acres are operated by the Northeast Iowa Farm Antique Association in an effort to preserve America's farming heritage. The barn is open during the Country Music Festival in June and the annual Old-Time Power Show the third weekend in September. Visitors to the power show can see demonstrations of agricultural equipment and household items more than 100 years old. Owners and collectors perform threshing, shredding, and rock-crushing chores with their equipment. Women make soap and wash clothes on old washboards and early washing machines. The smells of bread baking and apple butter cooking waft out of the summer kitchen. There are buggy rides, an antique tractor pull, tractor rodeo, and a horse pull, in addition to demonstrations of crafts such as candlewicking and butter churning. Two original log cabins and a stone mill are also on the site. Backtrack to US 52 and continue north to Guttenberg.

Just south of the town is a scenic overlook. The sign describes local geology:

> The high bluff on the west valley wall exposes the internal composition of the landscape into which the Mississippi entrenched its valley. These layered lime-stone strata muds are formed of much older deposits of lime-rich muds that accumulated in the shallow tropical seas that covered this area during the Ordovician time, approx. 440 million years ago. This bluff from here to the bottom of the hill contains the most complete exposure of the Galena group rocks known. This widespread rock sequence is named for outcrops at Galena, Illinois, and the term Galena refers to the lead ore which has been mined from this district for at least the last 300 years. These carbonate rocks also are characterized by numerous horizontal and vertical fractures and crevices. Through geologic time, some of these openings slowly enlarged by seeping ground-water. . . . The flow of moist, cool air through these subterranean passageways and out over valley slopes provides isolated rare habitats for unusual assemblages of plants normally found in more northern climates. This addition to the valley's offerings in earth history and ecological adaptation, this natural corridor was an important route of both prehistoric and historic exploration, trade, settlement and transportation.

The town of Guttenberg was originally explored by the French but was settled and named by German families in the early 1800s. The town is known for its natural beauty, with the high bluffs to the west and the broad, sweeping river to the east. Guttenberg, with its old river-facing brick buildings on the National Register of Historic Places, is home to a mile-long riverfront park, fifteen-mile bicycle trail, aquarium, several antique shops, a renovated 1850s-era brewery, and Lock and Dam No. 10, one of twenty-nine locks on the upper Mississippi River. Observation facilities allow visitors to watch boats lock through. This was among twenty-four locks approved by Congress in 1930 to deepen the channel for barges and towboats between Red Wing, Minnesota, and St. Louis, Missouri. Many Guttenberg residents helped to build the lock over its three-year construction at a cost of $4.8 million. The lock is 110 feet by 600 feet, and the dam is 1.2 miles long. The reservoir created is 32.8 miles long, and the navigation channel maintained at a minimum depth of nine feet is 1,000 feet wide. Lock No. 10 lifts or lowers watercraft eight feet between the two existing water levels. It takes about thirty minutes to perform a single lockage and seventy-five minutes for a multiple lockage, but only five minutes to raise or lower the water once the vessel is inside the lock. The lock performs more than 6,000 lockages a year, transporting some six million tons of grain, coal, oil, and chemical products. Adjacent to the lock is the Lockmaster's House Heritage Museum, the only remaining lockmaster house on the upper Mississippi. The museum recreates the furnishings of the lockmaster's house as it looked when constructed in 1938. Rooms include a sitting area, kitchen, bedroom, sewing room, and bath. A display on Lock and Dam No. 10 is in the basement.

At the town library, you can see a copy of the Gutenberg Bible, a facsimile copy of one of the original bibles, of which forty-six are known to exist today. The Gutenberg Bible, printed by Johannes Gutenberg, the inventor of moveable type, was the first book printed in the Western world.

You'll be able to cash in on local produce at the Farmers Market in Riverfront Park if you stop on Saturday mornings in the summer. We missed it, but we found plenty of antique shops in town to entertain my sister-in-law and myself. Try the Garage Antique Mall that features up to twenty-three dealers. Town House Accents, an antique and interiors shop, features the original tin ceiling and refinished maple floor from the 1886 building. Brochures describing self-guided tours, on foot or by car, of historic buildings are available at the Guttenberg Civic and Commerce Club.

West of downtown off US 52 at 407 South Bluff Street is an old limestone brewery built in 1858 by German settlers. The large structure was in disrepair when Naser and Patricia Shahrivar, two artists living in Cedar Rapids, fell in love with the site and bought it. "People thought we were crazy," said Patricia, "but look at it now." The two worked for several years to renovate it into an art gallery, bed and breakfast, and wine and beer tasting room. The two bed and breakfast rooms, featuring queen beds and private baths, are named Lucille and Viola after two daughters of the original brewery owner. The Shahrivars serve full breakfasts that may include blueberry waffles and sausage or French toast and hash-browns. The beer and wine room offers brews and vintages from Iowa's Amana Colonies. Although the old brick kilns had to be removed because they were in such bad condition, visitors can view the underground arched limestone caves where the beer was stored. The Shahrivars paint in a studio on the premises and display their wildlife art and cityscapes of river towns in the gallery.

German Fest, held late in September, celebrates the town's German heritage with authentic German food, beer, folk dancing, harmonica band, and the Guttenberg German Band. Continue north on US 52 to Garnavillo.

A handful of Garnavillo's historic buildings have been preserved, thanks to the local historical society. Turn west onto Centre Street, and you will see an original log cabin in the town park. The one-room structure, found on a nearby farm and reconstructed in the municipal park, contains furniture and dishes from the family of Judge Elias Williams. Across the street is a lodge building built in 1860 by the International Order of Odd Fellows for the use of its members and other lodges. Around the corner is the museum, housed in the former Congregational Church built in 1866, which contains manuscripts dating back to 1750; it includes one of the two known newspapers reporting the death of George Washington (the other is kept at the Smithsonian Institution in Washington, D.C.), a mastodon bone found nearby, medical equipment used by a local doctor, equipment used by a local veterinarian, tools, guns, a model of the Motor Mill (see Chapter 4, Elkader, etc.), and paintings of birds by Althea Sherman, a local artist who had an observation tower built for her research and enjoyment. Our trip ends here, but you can pick up another route starting in Elkader (see Chapter 4) or McGregor (see Chapter 3).

In the Area

Be sure to phone ahead, because many attractions are only open seasonally.

Field of Dreams Movie Site (Dyersville): 319-875-8404

Ertl Toy Company (Dyersville): 319-875-2000

National Farm Toy Museum (Dyersville): 319-875-2727

Country Junction Restaurant (Dyersville): 319-875-7055

Dyer-Botsford Historical House (Dyersville): 319-875-2414

Basilica of St. Francis Xavier (Dyersville): 319-875-7325

Becker Woodcarving Museum (Dyersville): 319-875-2087

Dyersville Area Chamber of Commerce (Dyersville)
     319-875-2311

Baum's Bed and Breakfast (Dyersville): 319-875-8383

Colonial Inn (Dyersville): 319-875-7194

Kerper's Country Store (New Vienna): 319-921-2715

Heritage House Museum (New Vienna): 319-921-2620

Fenelon Place Elevator Company (Dubuque): 319-582-6496

Heritage Trail (Dubuque): 319-556-6745

Cable Car Square (Dubuque): 319-583-5000

Dubuque Museum of Art (Dubuque): 319-557-1851

Woodward Riverboat Museum (Dubuque): 319-557-9545

Port of Dubuque Iowa Welcome Center (Dubuque):
   319-556-4372

Spirit of Dubuque (Dubuque): 800-426-5591

Five Flags Theater (Dubuque): 319-589-4254

Harbor Place Mall (Dubuque): 319-582-9227 or 582-0148

Mathias Ham House Historic Site (Dubuque): 319-557-9545

Dubuque Arboretum/Botanical Gardens (Dubuque):
   319-556-2100

St. Luke's United Methodist Church (Dubuque):
   319-582-4543

Redstone Inn (Dubuque): 319-582-1894

Hancock House (Dubuque): 319-557-8989

Dubuque Convention and Vistors Bureau (Dubuque):
   319-557-9200 or 800-798-4748

Breitbach's Country Dining (Balltown): 319-552-2220

Lockmaster's House Heritage Museum (Guttenberg):
   319-252-2323

Garage Antique Mall (Guttenberg): 319-252-3401

The Old Brewery Art Gallery and Bed and Breakfast
   (Guttenberg): 319-252-2094

Guttenberg Civic and Commerce Club (Guttenberg):
   319-252-2068

Garnavillo Historical Society (Garnavillo): 319-964-2185

6 ~

Davenport to Dubuque along the Great River Road

From Des Moines: Take I-80 east to the Quad Cities.

From Dubuque: Take US 61 south to the Quad Cities; or head south on US 52 and do the trip in reverse order.

Highlights: *Buffalo Bill Cody Homestead, Buffalo Bill Museum, Walnut Grove Pioneer Village,* Quad City Queen, *village of East Davenport, Hauberg Indian Museum, Clinton Area Showboat Theatre, Clinton County Historical Society Museum, Eagle Point Nature Center,* Mississippi Belle II; *Costello's Old Mill Gallery, Maquoketa Caves, Potter's Mill, Bellevue Butterfly Garden, Spring Side Inn Bed and Breakfast, Young Museum, other bed and breakfasts, historic village of St. Donatus. Allow at least two days for the entire trip.*

This trip follows the Great River Road from the Quad Cities north to Dubuque with a jog inland to Maquoketa and back up to Bellevue. Along the way, you will see several impressive views of the Mighty Mississippi with its towboats and massive barges, a reminder of the important role the river played in settlement, trade, and transportation in this part of Iowa in the 1800s. Our trip begins in Davenport, admittedly one of the state's largest cities, but the area contains important aspects of early country life and history of the area.

75

On an anguishing occasion in 1836, three years after defeat in the Black Hawk War, the Sauk and Fox nations convened in what is now the village of East Davenport to permanently sign over their land to the white settlers. As the tour guide paused, one silver-haired woman spoke up, "Can you imagine? Being defeated by invaders and then being booted off the land that had been home to your family for generations? We've treated the Indians terribly." A pin on her lapel said "Travel and Learn." She shook her head sadly as she walked down the street with her seniors group. During the next decade, the area became known as "Stubbs Eddy" because Capt. James R. Stubbs was stationed across the river at what is now the Rock Island Arsenal. Ironically, this brilliant officer from West Point who helped push the Indians off their land and prepare the way for white settlement, resigned his army post to live for eight years in a cave, closer to nature. In 1856 a railroad bridge spanning the river between Davenport and Rock Island was built; the log trestle still stands in the village of East Davenport as a reminder of the days when sawmills shipped cut lumber west by rail. Much of the village was built in the 1850s. When the Civil War began, the eastern part of the village was made into an army training camp called Camp McClellan. During the third weekend in September, the village holds a Civil War Muster and Mercantile Exposition when Civil War battles are recreated, artisans demonstrate their skills, and a military ball is held.

Today, several of the more than 500 homes and buildings have been renovated into shops, art galleries, and restaurants in this 120-acre district. With my interest in color, texture, and fibers, I found one of the most interesting to be The Fiber Shop, 2218 East Eleventh Street, with classes and supplies for knitting, weaving, crocheting, and basketry. On the other side of the village is the Garden Walk at Cothart Cottage, 2012 East Eleventh Street, offering tours of gardens in the village. I strolled past the yellow cottage through the garden, with its terraces and pathway that meanders up the hill. Nearby, stunning old homes sit atop the bluffs overlooking the Mississippi River.

For an overview of regional history, including Chief Black Hawk, Antoine LeClaire, and George Davenport, founders of the Iowa Quad Cities, visit the Putnam Museum of History and Natural Science, at Twelfth and Division Streets in Davenport. It features exhibits on natural history, the John Deere Company, and a live Heritage Theatre. The Colonel Davenport House on Arsenal Island is where George Davenport and Antoine LeClaire platted the city of Davenport. Later Davenport was surprised by river bandits who murdered him in his home. Across the river on a 208-acre natural area in Rock Island is the Hauberg Indian Museum, illustrating the life of the Sauk and Fox Indians during the time of Chief Black Hawk (1767–1838). The Rock Island Arsenal Museum on Arsenal Island depicts the history of Arsenal Island, the Black Hawk War, Confederate prison camp, and the establishment of the arsenal in 1862.

For great views of the Mississippi, see the Mississippi River Visitor Center on Arsenal Island where you can watch barges and towboats lock through Lock and Dam No. 15, and the Mississippi Valley Welcome Center, which looks like a riverboat captain's home. If that's not enough, take a river cruise; call the *President Riverboat Casino*. Head north out of the Quad Cities on US 67 to LeClaire.

The Buffalo Bill Museum in LeClaire, William Cody's birthplace, features a very good collection of memorabilia from his life and steamboat era artifacts. The *Lone Star*, the dry-docked, last-working, steam-driven, paddle-wheel towboat on the upper Mississippi, is open for a look. You can take a lovely and relaxing, old-time riverboat cruise departing from LeClaire to Galena, Illinois. Continue north on US 67 to Princeton, turn left onto County F33 (Bluff Road), and follow the signs for five miles to the Buffalo Bill Cody Homestead.

As I drove down the gravel road, the farmhouse, sitting on a little knoll overlooking the prairie where buffalo, burros, and longhorn cattle still graze, appeared lonely and deserted. I was surprised to find the two-story limestone house open. Information and photographs are posted in an enclosed back porch. Isaac Cody, Buffalo Bill's father, built the house in 1847. A photograph of Bill, as a two-year-old in a white dress, contrasts with others of the masculine bullwhacker, Pony Express rider, and scout. The house is furnished with nineteenth century antiques and memorabilia from Buffalo Bill, the government scout and Wild West showman. The parlor features a Galena daybed and wall-to-wall "carpet" of woven rags. As I looked at lacy dresses hanging in the closets and beautifully carved chests of drawers, I wondered how the house stayed intact with no apparent security. But as I walked out the back door, I was met by a uniformed worker. "Howdy, ma'am," he said. "Enjoy the house?" I told him that I felt relieved to know that there was someone around here. "Oh, yeah, we do a pretty good job of keeping an eye on the place," he answered. When you leave, turn left for .25 mile, left again on St. Anne's Road, and follow the signs for nearly five miles to Walnut Grove Pioneer Village at Long Grove.

Walnut Grove Pioneer Village contains nearly twenty renovated nineteenth century buildings including a blacksmith shop, train depot, mercantile, the Bison Saloon, fire station, postal and telegraph office, and the beautiful St. Anne's Church. The Ehlers Blacksmith Shop operated for almost 100 years at this site. The carpenter shop features a sign, "Coffins Made To Order." A young couple laughed as they read a combination sign: "Cobbler Shop and Saddlery/Tonsorial Parlor." The Butler Township Schoolhouse is representative of the more than 5,000 one-room schoolhouses prevalent in Iowa during the 1800s. There are also two log cabins in the village. A newspaper account in the old bank tells the story of a daring bank holdup on December 16, 1921, in Long Grove in which $5,000 was stolen, bandit Ray Purple died, and thirty-six shots were fired in the shootout. From here, go south to the next major intersection, then east to US 67 and north along the Great River Road to Clinton.

Clinton's history is inextricably tied to the river. The town grew up on transportation and lumbering during the late 1800s, and it is still an industrial area. You can enjoy the area's history through productions of the Clinton Area Showboat Theatre, professional summer theater on a paddle-wheel showboat dry docked in the town's Riverview Park. Cruises aboard the *Mississippi Belle II*, a paddle wheeler offering live entertainment, meals, and casino gambling, depart from Riverview Park for lunch, dinner, sight-seeing, or moonlight cruising. The Van Allen Building, 200 Fifth Avenue South, was designed by Louis Sullivan in 1914 as the Van Allen Department Store and is now a Sullivan museum archive and community center. The Curtis Mansion, 420 Fifth Avenue South, is the restored Victorian residence of lumber baron George M. Curtis. Curtis was one of the founders of the Curtis Brothers Company, which made window sashes, interior and exterior millwork, and doors. The mansion features the company's decorative interior millwork. The three-story, Queen Anne–style home built in 1883 features brick veneer with terra cotta decoration. It is a fine example of period architecture with Tiffany glass windows, carved banisters, and ten elaborate fireplaces.

The Clinton County Historical Museum in Root Park off Twenty-fifth Avenue North tells the story of the early lumber industry and early settlers. The collection includes a unique Victorian lingerie display, kitchen and farm tools, and period furniture. The Bickelhaupt Arboretum, 340 South Fourteenth Street, is an open-air museum of trees, shrubs, and flowers that was started by Frances and Robert Bickelhaupt on the grounds around their home. Among others, it contains exhibits of roses, lilacs, viburnums, flowering crabapples, a miniprairie, and ornamental shrubs.

On your way out of town, be sure to stop at the Eagle Point Nature Center, north side of the city and east of US 67, with impressive views of the Mississippi. The forty-acre natural area includes well-marked trails, a prairie demonstration area planted with native prairie flowers and native grasses, an authentic one-room schoolhouse, and an interpretive nature center. While I was there, a young woman photographed a little girl in an old-fashioned bonnet and long dress against the prairie background. It could have been Laura Ingalls sitting amongst the black-eyed Susans and purple coneflowers.

Continue north on US 67. At the intersection with State 64, stop at this pristinely white re-creation of a one-room schoolhouse—there were some 147 in the county—that is an Iowa Welcome Center with brochures and a gift shop. The first floor is furnished with desks and other school memorabilia. From there, head east on State 64 for a little detour to a quaint island.

Sabula is a small river town, which, after locks and dams raised the river level, is now an island town. You must drive over a bridge or causeway to reach it. The first settler had a more difficult arrival; he came in 1835 by floating on a log across the river. Sabula feels almost southern; the branches of trees droop down into the water, fishing boats rock lazily in the small marina. You could almost smell catfish and hushpuppies frying in a cast-iron skillet. Sabula thrived during the 1870s when good landings made it a convenient freight stop for steamships. There is a handful of shops, including some antique shops, in the town. The Castle Bed and Breakfast, 616 River Street, is a ninety-year-old stone-faced home on the river (they welcome children). South of town is South Sabula Lakes Park, a small county park right on the water, which offers good fishing and camping, an idyllic place in the summer. Head west on State 64.

About a mile before you enter Maquoketa, you will see Costello's Old Mill Gallery on the south side of the highway. In 1978 Patrick J. Costello, a nature lover and one-time staff artist for the *Quad-City Times*, with his wife bought the 1867 stone mill that had once been a flour and feed mill. They faced a monumental task—for fifty years it had been used as a horse barn, and the first floor had rotted away. With the artistic vision apparent in the wildlife paintings Patrick produces, the Costellos renovated the mill into a gallery, studio, gift shop, and living quarters. The day I arrived, you could see your breath floating in the frosty morning. The heavy front door creaked shut, and the warmth and smell of strong coffee drew me inside the old mill. Polished wood floors gleamed around an exhibit showing how millstones grind grain into flour. Several rooms contain wildlife paintings, landscapes, and a framing area. In a little nook at the rear of the building, I spied the coffee near a sprawling table. Nearby, a sign directs browsers outside to a small gift shop in the silo. The raised walkway to the silo looks down over a small meadow, grass-green in the mid-morning light, with tiny springs gurgling around it and the river running alongside it. I would trade, in an instant, my dream Victorian mansion to live here in this sublimely rural setting in this old stone mill. Continue west on State 64.

On the outskirts of Maquoketa, you will find the Jackson County Historical Museum at the fairgrounds. The "Hall of History" encompasses more than 23,500 square feet of exhibits including a working print shop, an old creamery, a country school, farm implements, quilts and textiles, toys, Victorian furnishings, and military artifacts. Continue on into town.

Maquoketa was settled in 1836 by J. E. Goodenow and Lyman Bates. Early businesses were Goodenow's Corn

Cracker and McCloy's flour mill. Later, it fostered businesses such as woolen mills, breweries, furnituremakers, cigar makers, wagon and pumpmakers, and foundries. The name came from a Sauk and Fox term meaning "there are bears." Don't worry if you have trouble spelling it—records kept by postal clerks show that mail has been received and delivered with "Maquoketa" spelled more than 1,000 different ways. Today, the town, population 6,000, features a thriving little business district and an historic district. The Old City Hall Gallery, on Olive and Pleasant Streets, was once a fire station, police station, and city hall.

If you want to stay in Maquoketa, consider Squiers Manor Bed and Breakfast, 418 West Pleasant Street in the West Pleasant Street Historic District. The district is bounded on the east by the 1904 Andrew Carnegie Maquoketa Free Public Library. The 1882 Queen Anne brick mansion, built by bank president J. E. Squiers, features a grand staircase of walnut and butternut. The house has three fireplaces and beautiful walnut, cherry, and butternut woodwork. It was the first house in town to have running water, thanks to an attic reservoir that collected rain water. There are six guest rooms with queen beds and private baths. Owners Virl and Kathy Banowetz, who own antique shops in Maquoketa and Galena, have furnished the house with American Victorian antiques. My accommodations were in the massive brick home of one of my college roommates, Bonnie Boulton Britten, her husband, Kent, and their four children. The Brittens always manage to find great old homes in Iowa towns, and Kent's pancakes are delicious. As Bonnie said, "All the comforts of home AND more children!" A brochure, "Historic Maquoketa," details some of the town's historic buildings and the West Pleasant Street Historic District.

From Maquoketa, take US 61 north, then head northwest on State 428 to the Maquoketa Caves State Park, where you can walk near rock formations, through limestone caves 1,100 feet deep, and under a naturally formed bridge. My five-year-old daughter and her two cousins loved exploring the eerie caves by flashlight and imagining spending winters there as some bands of Native Americans did. We enjoyed a picnic in the park before heading out. Go east on County E17 and then south on US 61 toward Maquoketa. About two miles before the town, you will see the Hurstville Lime Kilns, once part of a company town that made limestone from nearby hills and bluffs into lime for plaster and mortar. Alfred Hurst built the kilns in the 1870s in order to process an especially good grade of local limestone for his mortar business. At one time, fifty men worked to produce 1,000 barrels of fine lime per day. The town included a store, school, shipping point, post office, farming operation, blacksmith shop, and homes. The kiln included a barrel shop, a railroad spur, warehouses, and a stucco and brick manufacturing business. The business closed in the 1930s when Portland cement became widely used in the making of mortar. The kilns stood empty until they were restored by volunteers in 1985.

State 62 from Maquoketa to Bellevue leads first to Andrew, a small town with a restored, three-story limestone building that was the town jail. It features antique furniture, jailhouse graffiti, and jail cells. From Andrew, you can take a little side trip 6.3 miles east on County E17 to Springbrook, where you will find a quaint little general store. Gonners Store, on the National Register of Historic Buildings, is a grocery store, hardware store, clothing store, and post office. Backtrack to State 62. The route from Andrew to Bellevue follows an old frontier mail road. Just north of Andrew, the road winds through hills—the ridge gives you top-of-the-world views of the farms—and then descends into a wooded valley.

In prehistoric times, the Woodland Indians, and later the Sauk and Fox, Black Hawk's tribe, lived in the area known today as Bellevue. White settlers came around 1833 and started a town called Bell View; the spelling was changed to the French Belle Vue and later the words were merged into the current name. A freight train running through town forced me to wait or explore the immediate area, so I drove around and found several good examples of limestone architecture. After the train left, I could see that the main business area faces the river.

On the south side of Bellevue is Potter's Mill, built in 1843 by Elbridge Gerry Potter, along with the eleven-foot-thick dam. The twenty-foot-diameter waterwheel with buckets twelve feet wide powered the three burr stones and other equipment. Potter retired in 1871, and other owners changed the mill to keep up with technology. But when the mill closed in 1969, it had been in service 126 years. Dan and Daryll Eggers, with their wives Caroline and Carolyn, respectively, have restored the mill to its early flavor. Now it's a restaurant serving prime rib, roast pork, catfish, and trout, and a gift shop with quilts and country crafts.

Just across the creek is Bellevue State Park. A road is carved into the side of the limestone hill, and in autumn, I drove under a canopy of filtered sunlight and colored leaves that resembled stained glass. The high bluffs offer scenic views of the Mississippi. I strolled through the Bellevue Butterfly Garden to the sounds of crickets chirping, birds singing, and church bells peeling. Meadow and woodland trails wind past beds of coneflower, cosmos, zinnias, asters, pincushion flowers, ragweed, goldenrod, and milkweed, all planted to attract some sixty species of butterflies, either migrating or completing one of the stages of their life cycle. The park provides nectar plants for the adults and host plants for the caterpillars. Even in mid-October, there were a few butterflies. The South Bluff Nature Center features lifelike dioramas, natural history displays, and animal exhibits.

Farther south, off US 52 west on County Z15, are a house and two barns that once belonged to the Dyas family, believed to have come to the area before it was officially open for white settlement. The family built a cabin south of Bellevue. Others followed and built homes nearby. The George Dyas House is the westernmost of a group of houses and farm buildings known as the Dyas Farm. The limestone house built between 1850 and 1860 is one of the first limestone buildings in the county. The William Dyas Barn, still in use, is one of only nine still standing in the county. It was built during the 1850s. The Dyas Hexagonal Barn, built in 1921, also is still being used. Backtrack through town.

If you want to shop, Tomorrow's Keepsakes, 104 State Street, features porcelain dolls handmade by owner Sherri Michels. If you can't afford the few hundred dollars to buy a doll, it's still fun browsing. The Country Cupboard, 100 North Riverview, features homemade candies and antiques. The Young Museum, 410 North Riverview, which opened in 1966, is housed in a 100-year-old, ten-room home, built of native limestone. Decorated in turn-of-the-century and antique furnishings, it houses one of the world's best collections of Parian ware, as well as Haviland, Spode, and Limoge china. Mont Rest Bed and Breakfast, 300 Spring Street, an imposing structure built in 1893, is half-way up a nine-acre wooded bluff overlooking the Mississippi River. The mansion was built by Seth Baker in 1893 and lost two years later in a card game. The establishment offers five guest rooms decorated with antiques, homemade desserts, and a sumptuous country breakfast. If you can't stay over, make an appointment for a "Tea and Tour."

On your way out of town, you will see a distinctive Victorian home sitting on a hill to the west. It is the Spring Side Inn, named for the seven springs surrounding it. The home is an example of Gothic Revival architecture and was built of native limestone in 1850. Each guest room is named for a nineteenth century writer and features a volume or two of the author's works, a view of the river, queen-sized bed, and private bath.

Owners Mark and Nancy Jaspers "retired" from medical careers in Minneapolis to renovate the house and start a bed and breakfast business. Mark still teaches three days a week at the University of Iowa. He's also a fan of local history and entertained me with a synopsis of the "Bellevue War," a shootout between locals and a gang of counterfeiters and cattle rustlers. "Eight men were killed," he said. "That's more than in the more famous Western shootouts." Locals ended up capturing thirteen of the twenty-two crooks, tried them, and decided not to hang them. Instead they were whipped and "rivered," set adrift with provisions for three days on the river with no paddle for their boat. The punishment was not enough of a deterrent. "Two of them ended up four years later killing Colonel Davenport in Davenport," Mark explained. Continue north on US 52.

The highway runs right through St. Donatus, a village built by immigrants from Luxembourg. Driving into town from the south, I saw a church and a smaller chapel atop a nearby hill. I discovered that on Good Friday 700 to 1,000 penitents walk a path simulating Christ's Way of the Cross that winds up Calvary Hill from the St. Donatus Church to the little Pieta Chapel. The St. Donatus Church was built in 1858. Then in 1861 the Luxembourgers built the outdoor Way of the Cross with fourteen brick alcoves, with original Parisian lithographs of Christ's last walk. The Pieta Chapel was built in 1885.

Down in the village, Gehlen House and a barn are to the west and Kalmes Restaurant and Olde Tavern is to the east. Gehlen House was built in 1848 from limestone quarried in the area. After one historic building in town was torn down, Harold Fondell and his wife were determined not to let that happen again. "It was worth it," said Mrs. Fondell. "The house and the barn have so much history of the Luxembourger people. It would have been a shame to let them go." The twenty-room structure included a post office, trading post, grocery

The chapel built by Luxembourgian settlers in St. Donatus

store, and tavern on the main floor. The barn, made of hand-hewn beams and limestone, once included living quarters on the second story and pens for animals on the ground floor. The Fondells moved to a St. Donatus farm from Dubuque in 1961. "Harold is Luxembourger," she said. "And we just fell in love with this area." The Fondells refurbished the house to include a doll museum, tourist information area, and living quarters. The barn has been renovated for their antique shop.

87

The Kalmes family started in the early 1850s serving homecooked meals. Now the restaurant is run by the family's fourth generation. Over a bratwurst and sauerkraut sandwich, I enjoyed the warm, folksy ambiance of the dark little bar and restaurant. Men wearing caps with seed corn insignias sipped brews at the bar while they watched football overhead on TV and talked, sometimes in a Luxembourg dialect. At Oktoberfest the second weekend in October, you can sample some ethnic dishes such as *wiener schnitzel, tripen* (blood sausage), sour red cabbage, potato pancakes, homemade noodles, and *kwetzch* (plum) pie. And in January, Luxembourger language classes are held weekly at Kalmes Restaurant. Continue on US 52 and before you get to Dubuque, head southwest on State 151.

About fifteen miles southwest of Dubuque is the New Melleray Abbey, home of the Cistercian Trappist monks. The order was founded in the eleventh century by a small group of French monks who feared a weakening in the monastic rules. In the seventeenth century, they became known as the congregation of Our Lady of La Trappe or Trappists. New Melleray was founded in the 1800s by a group of monks from Ireland. The Trappists today have relaxed the strictest vows of silence and austerity. The Abbey includes 3,000 acres of farmland, and the monks make and sell delicious caramels. I've had several boxes of the rich, buttery caramels, and they are as good as those my Grandma Wenger once made.

(Refer to Chapter 5 for information on attractions in Dubuque.)

In the Area

Phone ahead as several attractions are open only seasonally.

Quad City Convention and Visitors Bureau (Rock Island): 309-788-7800 or 800-747-7800

Village of East Davenport (Davenport): 319-322-1860

The Fiber Shop (Davenport): 319-322-3535

Garden Walk at Cothart Cottage (Davenport): 319-322-2840

Putnam Museum of History and Natural Science
(Davenport): 319-324-1933

Rock Island Arsenal Museum (Rock Island): 309-782-5021

Mississippi River Visitor Center (Davenport): 309-788-6412

Mississippi Valley Welcome Center (LeClaire): 800-933-0708
or 319-289-3009

President Riverboat Casino (Davenport): 800-BOAT-711 or
319-322-BOAT

Buffalo Bill Museum (LeClaire): 319-289-5580 or 289-5447

River Cruises (LeClaire): 815-777-1660 or 800-331-1467

Buffalo Bill Cody Homestead (Princeton): 319-225-2981

Walnut Grove Pioneer Village (Long Grove): 319-381-1114 or
319-285-9903

Clinton Convention and Tourism Bureau (Clinton):
319-242-5702

Clinton Area Showboat Theatre (Clinton): 319-242-6760

Mississippi Belle II (Clinton): 319-243-9000 or 800-457-9975

Van Allen Building (Clinton): 319-242-2000

Curtis Mansion (Clinton): 319-242-8556

Clinton County Historical Society Museum (Clinton):
319-242-6797 or 242-4544

Bickelhaupt Arboretum (Clinton): 319-242-4771

Eagle Point Nature Center (Clinton): 319-243-1260

The Castle Bed and Breakfast (Sabula): 319-687-2714

Costello's Old Mill Gallery (Maquoketa): 319-652-3351

Jackson County Historical Museum (Maquoketa):
319-652-5030

Squiers Manor Bed and Breakfast (Maquoketa): 319-652-6961

Potter's Mill (Bellevue): 319-872-4237

Bellevue Butterfly Garden (Bellevue): 319-872-4019

Tomorrow's Keepsakes (Bellevue): 319-872-5771

The Country Cupboard (Bellevue): 319-872-3718

Young Museum (Bellevue): 319-872-4456

Mont Rest Bed and Breakfast (Bellevue): 319-872-4220

Spring Side Inn (Bellevue): 319-872-5452

Vander Veer Park and Conservatory (Davenport):
319-326-7818

7 ~

Steamboat Days in Southeastern Iowa

From Cedar Rapids: Take I-380 and US 218 south from Cedar Rapids.

Highlights: *Midwest Old Threshers' Reunion and Heritage Museums, Museum of Repertoire Americana, Mason House Bed and Breakfast, Manning Hotel, Bonaparte's Retreat, Liz Carson Cooking School, grand mansions of Keokuk, the Grande Anne Bed and Breakfast, Old Fort Madison, Heritage Hill, and West Jefferson National Historic Districts, and Snake Alley. Allow two to three days for this trip.*

Even though it's a four-lane highway, the drive south from Cedar Rapids is a rural and scenic one. The highway threads its way through woods and pastures. In autumn, the rolling hills are ablaze with color. Farther south, approaching Henry County, the terrain flattens. Farther south and east, approaching the Des Moines and Mississippi Rivers, the land rises and falls in hills, valleys, and bluffs. Our trip through southeastern Iowa evokes memories of the mid to late 1800s and early 1900s with images of old steamboats, the early railroads, and villages bustling with steamboat and rail passengers and trade for the mills and shops.

Swedesburg, in the northern part of the county, is small, but its Swedish heritage is pervasive. The immigrant farmers who arrived from Sweden in the 1870s are honored in the Swedish Heritage Museum. It includes artifacts and memorabilia from Sweden and early Swedish settlements and a genealogical library. Allow time to enjoy the Swedish pastries at Kaffe Stuga next door. If that's not enough, stay at the Carlson House Bed and Breakfast behind the museum, where Ruth, of Swedish descent, and Ned Ratekin offer two guest rooms with private baths in the 1918 home in which Ruth's mother was born and reared. The house features a comfortable Old World look, but "it's not like a museum," Ruth explains. The full breakfast features Swedish touches that may include Swedish rye bread, a tea-ring, almond toast, lingonberries, Swedish pancakes, or a baked *pfanakakke* (pancake). Continue south on US 218.

Mount Pleasant, a thriving town of 8,500 that is best known for the Midwest Old Threshers' Reunion, fans out from a picturesque town square. Several historic buildings face the square where, on summer weekends, visitors and residents dance in the streets or sit in their lawn chairs and listen to band concerts. Just meander down a few residential streets, and you will see that the town features many restored homes, including several Italianate and Queen Anne styles.

Mount Pleasant also is home to Iowa Wesleyan College, established in 1842, the oldest co-educational liberal arts college west of the Mississippi. Two of the most historical buildings on campus are Pioneer Hall built in 1845 and Old Main, a Georgian-style building built in 1855. Some of the rooms in Old Main have been restored in honor of the founding of the PEO Sisterhood, a women's philanthropic organization founded by seven women undergraduates at Iowa Wesleyan in 1869. The campus also contains the Harlan-Lincoln Museum, the 1860s home of James Harlan, once president of the college, U.S. senator, and secretary of the interior. President

Lincoln's son married the daughter of Senator Harlan, and the Lincoln family visited there. The historic home, open only by appointment, features many things from these two families including Mrs. Lincoln's mourning veil and a piece of her husband's coat, which he wore the night he was assassinated at Ford's Theater in Washington, D.C.

The Midwest Old Threshers' Reunion, held the five days ending Labor Day, is a hands-on history lesson depicting rural life as it evolved for thousands of farm families living in the mid- to late 1800s and early 1900s. The reunion features exhibits, Iowa's largest working craft show, villages illustrating life at the time, top-name country entertainment, and plenty of homecooked food provided by members of several local churches. The reunion features more than 100 operating steam engines, more than 300 antique tractors, and some 800 gasoline engines. The first reunion occurred in 1950 when a handful of enthusiasts met at the county fairgrounds to display fifteen steam engines and eight separators. These "smoke-belching behemoths" powered a number of farm activities until the gasoline-powered tractor came along in the 1920s. Now the reunion is held on a 160-acre site filled with museums, a gift shop, a narrow-gauge railroad, operating antique trolleys, and a sixty-acre campground. Almost anything that was once a part of rural or small-town America can be found here. Hundreds of exhibits include antique automobiles, craft demonstrations, and the old ways of making necessities, such as soap. In the Midwest Village, you can attend classes in a one-room schoolhouse, sing in a church hymn-sing, and buy "goods" at the general store. In the Log Village, where Explorer Scouts re-enact pioneer life in Iowa in the 1840s, you will find a general store, stagecoach inn, buckskinners encampment, and garden.

Lennis Moore, administrator of the Reunion and himself an artist, showed us around the Heritage Museums, three acres of antique tractors, old steam traction engines, other

A steam thresher at the Midwest Old Threshers' Reunion

farm machinery and tools, and interpretive exhibits on rural electrification, water power, and women's contributions to the family farm. The newest is a display of a 1939 machine shop that looks as if the workers just left for lunch. At the far end of the building, a man repairs some trim on one of the trolleys. "It's really the volunteers who make the Reunion happen," said Moore. The exhibits did just what they were designed to do: my dad reminisced about the electric light plant on the family farm, and my mother found an old Hoosier cabinet similar to one that my grandmother had used. Soon they were telling bits and pieces of family history that I hadn't heard before.

Also on the grounds is the Museum of Repertoire Americana, which contains one of, if not THE largest collection of America's early-day tent, folk, repertoire, theater, and opera memorabilia. Exhibits come from the days when chautauqua and lyceum companies, medicine and minstrel shows, and tent and repertoire theater companies performed in hundreds of opera houses and town halls, as well as more than 400 tent theaters for rural audiences. The two-story brick building includes thousands of costumes, play scripts, photographs, advertisements, newspaper clippings, scripts, and an impressive collection of opera house curtains, hand-painted canvas backdrops used in the many plays. The museum was the dream of Neil and Caroline Schaffner, former owners of the Schaffner Players and originators of the characters Toby and Susie, a country boy and his sharp-tongued girlfriend.

Head south on US 218, and at County J20 you can head east to Geode State Park. Six miles south of New London is Geode State Park in the eastern part of Henry County. The park is named after the geode stone, native to the area, which attracts many rock hounds. In addition, there is fishing, swimming, a boat ramp, canoe and boat rentals, hiking on developed nature trails, and camping. Backtrack, crossing US 218 and heading west to Salem.

Residents of early Salem, a mostly Quaker settlement, are said to have transported more slaves through the town than any other in the state during the abolitionist movement. A stone house built by Henderson Lewelling in the early 1840s, which was part of the Underground Railroad, features exhibits such as leg irons and other equipment from people running away from slavery. Follow County J20 west, and at Hillsboro, go south to State 16. Head west and follow the signs to Bentonsport, the first of the three villages of Van Buren County that we will visit.

The villages are only memories of what they once were. In the mid-1800s, the Des Moines River was a thriving "country road," with steamboat traffic pouring up and down the river catering to the mills, stores, and hotels in the bustling port towns along the way. Then the federal government announced that it would no longer maintain the locks and dams that allowed the big riverboats to navigate. This spelled near-death to the once active towns. More recently, some of the villages have experienced a bit of a revival with some historic restoration, renovation, and a few new businesses. While water once enabled these towns to boom, it also can be the bane of their existence. The corner of the Mason House was hit by a tugboat during a flood in 1851. A 1947 flood left the owner and guests in Keosauqua's Hotel Manning sleeping on the second floor and using a rowboat to get across the hotel lobby. More recently, floods in 1993 invaded buildings in several areas and demolished a lovely rose garden in Bentonsport. Nevertheless, indefatigable Iowans are working to replant it.

A handful of historic buildings and a boardwalk facing the waterway evoke memories of the riverboat era in the near-ghost town of Bentonsport, named for Sen. Thomas Hart Benton of Missouri. The village had the state's first paper mill, a flour mill, a handful of churches, a school, and a slate of social activities including dances, concerts, and steamboat races. The Georgian-style Mason House, built by Mormon craftsmen en route to Utah, was once THE overnight stop for steamboat passengers. The hotel, open for tours, is decorated with romantic lace curtains and antiques, including an eight-foot recitation school desk, an 1875 map of the county, an 1882 Esty pump organ, and some original furnishings. The hotel is now connected with an old railroad station building, allowing for private accommodations on the first floor. Sheral and Bill McDermet offer a cookie jar in every guest room and meals by reservation. Down the street, a handful of buildings, including the Federal-style Greef General Store, the largest store in the county at one time, house antiques and arts and crafts. At the end of the street is Iron & Lace blacksmith/pottery shop. "We built it in 1990 with 100-year-old posts, beams, and siding collected from old barns," said blacksmith Bill Printy, who forges iron into utilitarian fireplace tools and decorative pieces. Iron and Lace also sells Betty Printy's distinctive pottery, pressed with delicate Queen Anne's lace wildflowers. Head west on County J40 and north on State 1 to Keosauqua.

Keosauqua is the native word for "big bend," which aptly describes its location on the horseshoe bend of the Des Moines River. The Hotel Manning, a symbol of the steamboat era, is the town's best known landmark. Built initially as a one-story general store and bank, it was transformed into a hotel in the 1890s with the addition of the second and third stories. A veranda on the first two stories stretches the length of the building, and the eighteen guest rooms are individually decorated featuring antiques. One of the hotel's most distinguished guests was T. S. Eliot. The spacious lobby features fourteen-foot ceilings, original woodwork, large open staircase, and antique fixtures. The hotel was named for settler Edward Manning who arrived in the area in 1837, built a log cabin trading post, and helped found the town. Across the river from the hotel, bordering the big bend, is the 1,600-acre Lacey-Keosauqua State Park, the site of Ely Ford where Mormons crossed the river on their way west. Today, the park offers cabins, hiking trails, and canoeing.

The oldest home in town is Bonneyview at 12 Third Street, built between 1837 and 1840, with an excellent view of the river. The Pearson House at the corner of Dodge and Country Roads was built half-stone and half-brick in 1847. Once a stop on the Underground Railroad, the house hid runaway slaves in a secret room that still exists in the cellar. The county historical society maintains the structure and offers tours. The Federal-style Van Buren County Courthouse is the state's oldest courthouse in continuous use, starting in 1840. The original courtroom has been restored and, when court is not in session, is open for tours. The courthouse was the scene of the first death sentence in the state; the hanging occurred nearby in Hangman's Hollow.

About two miles west of Keosauqua in the town of Pittsburg is the birthplace of Phil Stong, author of *State Fair*, which was made into three films. Stong, born in 1899, had covered the state fair as a reporter for the *Des Moines Register*, and his grandfather had been superintendent of the swine division at the fair. He wrote the book at his wife's suggestion, and it became an immediate success. He went on to write more than forty novels, many of which are set in the Van Buren area. Backtrack to Keosauqua, south on State 1 and east on State 2 to Bonaparte.

The old woolen and grist mill town of Bonaparte features quaint historic structures. In 1987 the residents started renovating and restoring the buildings that make up the small downtown, along Main Street, First Street, and Washington Street, now a National Historic District. Bonaparte's Retreat, one of the area's best restaurants, is housed in an 1878 grist and flour mill with two-foot-thick beams, a walnut-backed bar, antique quilts, and mill memorabilia. The old woolen mill is an antique shop. At the corner of Second and Washington Streets is the Aunty Green Museum, built in 1844, now a museum and city library. The town, originally called Meeks Mills, was founded in 1837. The mills attracted other businesses and new residents, and eventually the woolen mill enjoyed an international reputation for producing fine woolens. A dam was built across the river for use by the mills. Later, in 1846, another dam and lock, this one of stone masonry, was built to improve navigation on the river; part of the lock, which now contains a butterfly garden, can still be seen in Riverfront Park. Visitors to the town during the 1800s included outlaw Jesse James, composer Anton Rubinstein, and

Chief Black Hawk. Continue east on State 2, just past Farmington.

Shimek State Forest, the largest contiguous stand of state-owned forest, includes 9,000 acres of hickory, oak, and pine trees planted by the Civilian Conservation Corps near Farmington where visitors can hike, camp, fish, cross-country ski, snowmobile, and enjoy horse trails. Continue east on State 2 and south on State 218 to Keokuk.

Located at the confluence of the Des Moines and Mississippi Rivers, Keokuk lies in the most southeasterly portion of Iowa. It is named for Chief Keokuk of the Sauk/Fox Indians. After white settlers arrived, the city flourished as a hub for steamboats, railroads, and manufacturing. During its early days, Keokuk literally was the jumping-off place for steamboat travelers, who had to disembark and continue their journey on land or board another boat farther upriver, because steamboats were unable to continue past this point. One of the town's notable residents was Mark Twain, who worked on a newspaper here.

On the way into town, you will see signs for the National Cemetery. At the same time Congress designated Arlington National Cemetery, it designated Keokuk National Cemetery, one of the original twelve and the only national cemetery in Iowa. Soldiers from both sides in the Civil War and representatives of every military conflict since are buried here. During the Civil War, Keokuk had seven hospitals for wounded men shipped up the Mississippi River from the South. Head through downtown, much of which looks as if it has seen better days, to the riverfront.

What better location for the Keokuk River Museum than the Mississippi stern-wheel towboat, the *George M. Verity?* Docked on the river in Victory Park at the end of Main Street, the boat features river memorabilia and photographs of old riverboats. The boat was one of four built in 1927 to revive shipping on the Mississippi. Head over to the Keokuk

Hydroelectric Power Plant and Lock 19. When it was built in 1913, the power plant was the world's largest. The 1,200-foot-long lock is the largest on the upper Mississippi.

The lock and dam are responsible for one of Keokuk's off-season attractions, hundreds of bald eagles who feed in the unfrozen water below the dam. The city hosts Bald Eagle Appreciation Days the third weekend in January, with a listing of best viewpoints, lectures, films, and exhibits on the magnificent birds.

Cross the Mighty Mississippi on the Hamilton-Keokuk Bridge, and imagine the engineering it took to build this structure. (From here, you can take a side trip north on Illinois State 96 to Nauvoo, Illinois) Head back into Keokuk for a glimpse of what must have been boom times for the town.

The Samuel F. Miller House and Museum, once home of U.S. Supreme Court Justice Samuel F. Miller appointed by Abraham Lincoln, is located at 318 North Fifth Street. The restored and refurbished home features displays on local, state, and national history.

Take a scenic drive on Grand Avenue past the opulent mansions on the bluff overlooking the river. Brochures are available with information on the various architectural styles from the Civil War era to Victorian and turn-of-the-century times.

Along the way, you will see the Grande Anne Bed and Breakfast, 816 Grand Avenue. This twenty-two-room Queen Anne–Revival home was built in 1897 for Clyde Royal Joy, national director of the YMCA. One of the later owners was Judge W. Logan Huiskamp. An outstanding example of painstaking restoration, the Victorian home features two parlors, a music room, formal dining room, kitchen, and three guest rooms, each furnished with antiques. Judge Huiskamp's suite offers spectacular views of the river. The owners' love of aviation and antique toys is evident throughout the house.

Guests will enjoy fresh-baked cookies and apple cider at bed-time, a fruit basket in the room, and a full, gourmet breakfast.

Another mansion worth savoring is Liz Clark's gourmet restaurant and cooking school, 116 Concert Street. Liz Clark's resulted from the necessity of funding her house habit. A native of the area, she bought her nineteenth century Italianate mansion for a song, but "I had to supplement my teaching salary to fund the renovation," she said. She combined her love of good food with what she'd learned about cooking in France and Italy and opened her own private restaurant in 1976. That, and her cooking school, which opened later, have earned her a national reputation.

The Sampler House Tea Room, 120 North Fourth Street, a two-story brick Italianate house, looks like one of the houses featured in the old cross-stitched samplers. Everything on the changing menu is made fresh from scratch, and the desserts are so popular, guests often order them first, just to make sure they don't run out. If almond cream cake or pecan pie don't tempt you, the gift shop will.

High on a bluff overlooking the river in Rand Park is the burial site of Chief Keokuk, of the Sauk/Fox Indians. You'll find fabulous views of the river and surrounding countryside, as well as lovely flower gardens.

After enjoying the park, drop down on the scenic drive on River Road for about two miles past small boats and bait shops. Turn left onto Middle Road, which winds back through hills, trees, and farmland. Eventually you will come to a T-intersection. A left turn will take you back to US 218 and then US 61 north to Fort Madison.

Fort Madison was named for President James Madison, chief executive when the first U.S. military fort on the upper Mississippi was built here in 1808–09 to help protect the Louisiana Purchase, acquired in 1803, and to trade with the Indians.

Old Fort Madison, in Riverview Park, is an historically accurate replica of the fort, including a stockade, four block-houses, and several enclosed buildings, built there almost 200 years ago. It comes to life daily in the summer when inter-preters wearing costumes of the early nineteenth century recreate the history of the fort with booming cannons and cracking muskets. Outside the walls, a trading post offers gifts and publications. Most of the Indians were on friendly terms with the fort, but occasionally, groups of Sauk, Fox, and Winnebago, led in part by Sauk warrior Black Hawk, troubled the fort. During the War of 1812, the British persuaded the Sauk and Fox tribes to attack the fort, killing one soldier, slaughtering the cattle, and setting fire to cabins nearby. When they attacked again in 1813, killing six soldiers, the commander ordered his soldiers to abandon the fort. Under nightfall, they escaped by boat on the river and set fire to the fort, making it useless to the Indians. A blackened chimney was the remaining landmark.

In 1965 work in the parking lot of the W. A. Sheaffer Pen Company, the first company to make a practical, refillable fountain pen, uncovered part of the cellar from a blockhouse. More excavations revealed remnants of barracks, officers' quarters, and two other blockhouses. In 1983 prisoners at the Iowa State Penitentiary in Fort Madison began work to build a replica of the original fort using hand tools and techniques that would have been used to build the original fort. All the structures were built in the prison and then reassembled in Riverview Park, several blocks south of the original site, but in the same proximity to the Mississippi River. Riverview Park also contains the North Lee County Historical Center in the 1910 mission-style Santa Fe Railroad station. The center traces local history with exhibits of a Silsby steam pumper and hose cart, ice-gathering tools, railroad and farm equipment, prison cell, and arrowheads. The downtown riverfront features old buildings, many of which house antiques or secondhand stores. An old hotel has been renovated with Alpha's, a restaurant and lounge with old brick walls as a backdrop for country memorabilia, such as carpet beaters, candle molds, and butter churns. The hotel, now a bed and breakfast, features fourteen individually decorated rooms with antiques.

The Lee County Courthouse is the state's oldest. The Greek Revival–style structure was built in 1841.

Fort Madison offers a visual feast of stately Victorian homes; a driving tour brochure features information on eighty-nine of them. After that, cross the Santa Fe Bridge, the largest double-deck swingspan bridge in the world. It carries vehicular and train traffic and swings open to allow river traffic through. Opposite Fort Madison is Nauvoo, Illinois, once a city of 20,000 when it was headquarters for the Church of Jesus Christ of the Latter Day Saints. Although most of the Mormons left by 1847 after conflicts with other residents, the town is rich in history with more than twenty restored Mormon buildings, the Icarian Living History Museum, and remnants of vineyards planted by French, German, and Swiss settlers. Backtrack to Fort Madison and continue north on US 61 to Burlington.

On the way out of town, follow US 61. Phone ahead to get a tour of one of the best restored country schoolhouses in the state. When the highway takes a jog to the right (near a small antique shop), turn left. Continue four miles, past the prison farms, and you will come to Brush College, a one-room, red brick country schoolhouse sitting on a knoll. The school, circa 1861, has been restored to the 1897 period with desks built with square wooden pegs, a wooden water tub, log stove, teacher's desk, and McGuffy Readers. Albertine Winke, now in her eighties, who taught in rural schools for many years, spearheaded the restoration in the 1960s and has been leading tours of it ever since. Every spring, dressed in a schoolmarm's dress from 1897, she portrays the teacher for groups of schoolchildren who sit in the desks and write their lessons on the old slates. "I combed through schools all over the place looking for things from the 1897 period," she said. Ms. Winke made use of the keen mind of a teacher friend of hers who had been a rural schoolteacher in 1897. Pioneers named the school for the brush along the river and then made the name more distinctive by calling it a college instead of a school. Follow US 61, then go east on US 34, taking the Center Street exit into downtown Burlington.

The land around this area of the Mississippi was known to the Sauk and Fox tribe as "Shoquoquon," or flint hills. The settlement and statehood of Illinois in 1818 drove many Indians from their native lands. The Black Hawk Wars resulted. After the Indians were defeated, Iowa was opened for white settlement in 1833. It already had been visited by French explorers Father Jacques Marquette and Louis Joliet in 1673 and Zebulon Pike in 1805. President Thomas Jefferson had organized two parties of explorers to map out the Louisiana Purchase. Lewis and Clark followed the Missouri River, and Pike followed the Mississippi. A trading post was established in 1808. Burlington was the second capital of the Wisconsin Territory, from 1837 to 1838, and the first capital of the Iowa Territory, from 1838 to 1840. Its strategic location on the Mississippi made Burlington a leader in the development of the rest of the state.

The name Burlington came from John Gray after his home in Vermont. Water Street, which ran alongside the river, was the first area to be built upon. Earliest storefronts were wood and hastily thrown together. As the town expanded and prospered, and after a large fire in 1873, brick and stone buildings replaced wooden ones. The "main street" of most river towns paralleled the river, but Burlington's hills and the valley between them drew growth perpendicular to the river on Jefferson Street. Much of the development came after the Civil War and results from many influences including the river, railroad development, economic booms and busts, and

The Delta Queen *steams past Iowa's Mississippi bluffs*

the cultural diversity of the residents. The blocks 400-800 West Jefferson Street are a National Historic District, including forty-nine key buildings, most of which are two- and three-story structures of brick and sandstone. Many of the buildings are of the Italianate style, typical of those built after the Civil War. A brochure for a self-guided walking tour is available.

Burlington's riverfront shows evidence of its rowdy past and its teeming growth during the boom times of the steamboats. Between 1830 and 1860, steamboats provided strong economic ties with the East and South. The city's Municipal River Terminal, built in 1928, at a time when the levee was paved with cobblestones and the terminal was the largest cargo transfer point between St. Louis and Davenport, is now the Port of Burlington and an Iowa Welcome Center with interpretive exhibits and historic displays.

When rail traffic crossed the Mississippi, Burlington thrived. The completion, in 1868, of a railroad bridge across the river guaranteed the town's significance in east-west rail traffic. Cargo being transferred from boat to rail made the steamboat landing especially busy, and in 1879, the worn cobblestones had to be relaid. As the importance of river traffic diminished, the city's warehouse district shifted from the riverfront to inland streets, following trains heading west for Omaha. The Burlington, Cedar Rapids and Northern Railroad was established in 1867, but it failed after only a few short years. But with the Chicago, Burlington, and Quincy and the Rock Island lines, the railroad grew to become the largest north-south line in Iowa. The Freighthouse stands as a memorial to the city's importance in expansion of the railroad. The bridge was replaced by the current double-track bridge in 1892.

The city's downtown architecture illustrates its economic history. Italianate buildings of the late 1800s are shouldered by utilitarian structures of the Depression era, along with Chicago-style buildings and the futuristic appearance of Art Deco.

North of downtown is Heritage Hill, a National Historic District rich in architectural details. The twenty-square-block area includes about 160 buildings, including several churches located on the hillside buffer between the affluent residential area and the business district. Architectural styles include many features of Gothic Revival, Renaissance Revival, Italianate, Georgian Revival, Queen Anne, and Tudor Gothic. This area contains limestone curbs, limestone retaining walls, brick walks, cobblestone and brick alleys, and garden walls. Brochures for self-guided walking tours discuss the history of many architectural styles of the area, including Victorian, Greek, Gothic Revival, and Italian Villa. The Arts for Living Center, housed in an 1868 church in this historic district, offers classes, changing exhibits, sculpture garden, gift shop, and annual art fair.

Snake Alley is probably the best known element on Heritage Hill. In order to provide a more direct route from the residences atop the hill and the business district, an alley of switchbacks was built in 1894. The locally fired blue clay bricks were laid at an angle to give the horses better footing on the steep hillside. The curved limestone curbing edges the five half-curves and two quarter-curves over a distance of 275 feet from Columbia Street down 58.3 vertical feet to Washington Street.

The lifestyle of one of Burlington's prominent early families is illustrated in the Phelps House, furnished with possessions of three generations of the family. William Garrett, a dry goods merchant and bank cashier, built the original house, a two-story brick house with gabled roof, in 1851. An expansion in 1870 doubled its size, adding a third floor mansard roof reflecting a Second Empire style and an Italian Villa tower with double balconies. The nine rooms open to the public feature marble fireplaces, mahogany and walnut furniture, parquet floors with oriental carpets, family silver, china, and a rare set of yellow Wedgwood. One of the family portraits is of David Rorer, Mrs. Garrett's father, who originated the idea of nicknaming Iowa the "Hawkeye" state. The house was Burlington's first Protestant hospital for five years, starting in 1894. In that same year, Snake Alley was built adjacent to the house. The home and its contents were donated to the county historical society in 1974.

If you are looking for a splendid old home to enjoy, consider the Mississippi Manor, a bed and breakfast at 809 North Fourth Street, just north of US 34. The antebellum home features six ornate fireplaces, high ceilings, walnut and mahogany woodwork, splendid views of the river, and four guest rooms named after Mark Twain characters.

Follow Main Street south to Crapo Park. The site where Lt. Zebulon Pike first raised the U.S. flag on what was to become Iowa soil is marked by the Hawkeye Log Cabin, built in 1910 by members of the Hawkeye Natives Association, a group promoting friendship among people born in Iowa. The cabin features pioneer furnishings and tools used in early settlement. Continue west and take Madison Avenue north, west on Harrison Street, north on Central Street and west on Dill Street to Perkins Park.

The Apple Trees Museum is housed in an 1899 addition to the Charles E. Perkins mansion. Perkins came to Burlington as a clerk for the Burlington and Missouri River Railroad. He worked his way up to become president of the CB&Q Railroad. Perkins gave "The Garden of the Gods" to the city of Colorado Springs. He expanded what was once a small cottage into a mansion of several wings that included thirty-nine rooms. This wing is the only part of the house saved when the heirs gave the land to the city for a park. It features carved oak woodwork and large fireplaces. The museum includes a Victorian collection, Native American artifacts collected by Perkins, antique china, dolls, toys, needlework, and tools.

Thirteen miles north of Burlington on US 61 near Sperry, the family can enjoy Grandpa Bill's Farm, now a 100-acre park featuring a crafts barn, the "Iowa Proud" barn, children's play barn, hayrides, and the Barn Theatre with shows and home-made meals.

Our tour ends here. You can continue north on State 99 or US 61 toward the Quad Cities and the Great River Road.

In the Area

Phone ahead as several attractions are only open seasonally.

Swedish Heritage Museum US 218 (Swedesburg):
319-254-2317

Carlson House Bed and Breakfast (Swedesburg):
319-254-2451

Harlan-Lincoln Home (Mount Pleasant): 319-385-8021

Midwest Old Threshers' Heritage Museums (Mount Pleasant): 319-385-8937

Museum of Repertoire Americana (Mount Pleasant):
319-385-8937

Villages of Van Buren (Keosauqua): 319-868-7822 or
800-TOUR-VBC

Bentonsport National Historic District (Bentonsport):
319-293-7111

Mason House Bed and Breakfast (Bentonsport):
800-592-3133

Hotel Manning (Keosauqua): 319-293-3232

Van Buren County Courthouse (Keosauqua): 319-293-7111

Bonaparte National Historic District (Bonaparte):
319-592-3400

Bonaparte's Retreat (Bonaparte): 319-592-3339

Indian Lake Park and Shimek State Forest (Farmington):
319-878-3706

Keokuk Convention and Tourism Bureau (Keokuk):
319-524-5055 or 800-383-1219

Keokuk National Cemetery (Keokuk): 319-524-1304

Keokuk River Museum (Keokuk): 319-524-4765

Samuel F. Miller House and Museum (Keokuk):
319-524-7283

Grand Anne Bed and Breakfast (Keokuk): 319-524-6310

Liz Clark's (Keokuk): 319-524-4716

Sampler House Tea Room (Keokuk): 319-524-1581

Chief Keokuk Burial Site (Keokuk): 319-524-3272

Fort Madison Convention and Tourism Bureau (Fort
Madison): 319-372-5471 or 800-369-FORT

Old Fort Madison Historical Site (Fort Madison):
319-372-7700 or 319-372-6318

Riverview Park (Fort Madison): 319-372-7700 ext. 33

North Lee County Historical Center (Fort Madison):
319-372-7661

Brush College (Fort Madison): 319-372-2688

Burlington Convention and Tourism Bureau (Burlington):
319-752-6365

Port of Burlington Welcome Center (Burlington):
319-752-8731

Heritage Hill Historic District (Burlington): 319-752-6365 or
800-82-RIVER

Arts for Living Center (Burlington): 319-754-8069

Snake Alley Historic District (Burlington): 319-752-6365

Phelps House (Burlington): 319-753-2449

Hawkeye Log Cabin (Burlington): 319-753-2449

Apple Trees Museum (Burlington): 319-753-2449

Grandpa Bill's Farm (Sperry): 319-985-2262

8 ~

Country Stores, Dutch Gardens, and Wooden Shoes

From Des Moines: Go northeast on State 330 and north on State 14 to Conrad.

From Waterloo: Go south on US 63, west on State 175 and south on State 14 to Conrad.

Highlights: *Conrad General Store and Conrad Tea Room, State Center Rose Garden, Watson's Grocery Store, Matthew Edel Blacksmith Shop in Haverhill, Mesquakie Indian settlement near Tama, Jasper County Historical Museum and La Corsette in Newton, the Dutch town of Pella, the Historical Village, Scholte House, Pella Opera House. Allow two days for this trip.*

This is the stereotypical part of Iowa—the image most travelers carry with them long after they leave I-80: that Iowa is flat and full of cornfields, and they lump it with Kansas, Nebraska, and the Dakotas. To be sure, this central area contains some of the richest farmland in the world, and being able to drive the tractor in a long, straight line rather than weaving around hills and trees certainly improves agricultural efficiency, not to mention safety. (More than one northeast Iowa farmer has been injured when a tractor precariously balanced on a sidehill shifted its center of gravity and toppled over, pinning the driver beneath it. Blessed with this "black gold," farmers make the most of their acreages by growing vast fields of corn and soybeans. You will see few, if any, beef cattle or dairy herds. This trip starts in Conrad, which calls itself "Black Dirt Capital of the World," and ends in Pella, Iowa's premiere Dutch settlement and one of the prettiest towns in the entire state.

The first time my mother and I visited Conrad was on a Sunday afternoon when, to our disappointment, the General Store and the Briar Patch Tea Room were closed. Wistfully, we peeked through the windows of both and promised to return. After putting gas in the car, we ate pie and ice cream at the lunch counter of the service station, sort of a consolation. Conrad is the kind of place where even at "the station," the pie is homemade.

On our return a few days later, we treated ourselves to a teatime lunch at the Briar Patch Tea Room. Don't let this place confuse you—you must walk through the Country Inn, a more typical lunch place with formica tables, burgers, and other standard fare. (Both are owned by Bev Rabbitt.) Ask to be seated next door in the Tea Room, which is furnished with country antiques and memorabilia such as lace gloves with pearl buttons framed and hanging on the wall. There are at least three entree options. We enjoyed a chicken breast salad with fresh green grapes and a croissant. My tea came in a lovely china pot sitting on a matching oblong china plate. Mom drank her gourmet coffee from a gilt-edged cup and saucer. We had to forsake the desserts, which include cheese-cake and homemade pies and pastries, because we'd already raided two bakeries in Pella, but more about that later.

Across the street is the Conrad General Store, 101 North Main Street, which marks its centennial in 1994. "I remember coming here as a little girl with a shopping list from my mother," said Janice Juchems, the newest co-owner of the store. "I'd twirl around on one of the stools, while someone got the things together from the list." Some people come in to say they were last in the store forty years ago and spent a nickel for candy. Older people say they remember as children bringing in eggs for credit. The General Store was built in 1894 after a fire that destroyed most of the downtown. Brenda Shine, a Conrad farmwife, and Jeanne Zehr bought the store with its old oak and glass counters, original fixtures, and pine flooring. "There have only been three or four owners," said Shine, "So there haven't been many people carting things out of here." While it's called a general store, some would disagree. To wit: the day I was there, a man called to ask if they carried "mitten socks" (slipper socks). "Oh, dear, I had to tell him 'no,'" said Juchems. "We have discontinued carrying all the workclothes that the previous owner carried," said Shine. The shop is one of the best stocked with quilting fabrics, quilting stencils, books, patterns, lace by the yard for making curtains, and materials for craft projects. Gift items include corn husk dolls and Juchems's artistic arrangements of dried and silk flowers.

The Conrad General Store usually sponsors a quilt show in conjunction with "Black Dirt Days" the first weekend in August. Conrad calls itself the "Black Dirt Capital of the World." "I guess that's because Grundy County has some of the richest soil in the world," said Shine.

If you have more time and enjoy crafts, make an appointment with Marlyne's Palettable Gifts in rural Conrad. Although Marlyne is Danish, she "took to" the Norwegian art of rosemaling once she saw it at the Nordic Fest in Decorah. She offers classes, demonstrations to groups, and gifts ranging from $2 to $200. Head south on State 14 to Marshalltown.

Side trip: Take a diagonal, State 330, and then go west on US 30 to State Center, Rose Capital of Iowa. Here you will find a living memorial, the State Center Rose Garden, with more than 100 rose bushes, many of which are memorials to people who lived in and around the town. Others have been donated by nurseries. State Center's Rose Festival is the third weekend in June. Take a trip back in time to Watson's Grocery Store, 106 West Main Street, a restored mercantile and 1895 general store with oak cabinetry and original fixtures. The mercantile and grocery business started in 1882 and the Watson family bought it in 1885, according to Wilma Eckhart, a seventy-year-old member of the State Center Historical Society. Watsons moved the business into this building in 1895 and ran it until 1989. At that time, townspeople banded together, formed a committee, and bought the building. Volunteers run the store, mostly a museum, and sell a few souvenirs. On the shelves, you will see containers from bygone years, grocery items, and dry goods, such as old Wheaties cereal boxes and metal cans that once held spices, crackers, and cookies. There are the old-time barrels, cash register, a sausage stuffer, ice box, and a set of scales. Backtrack to State 14.

Side trip: Head east on US 30 to Tama and the Mesquakie settlement. The Tama Pow Wow exhibits traditional ceremonies that express Mesquakie religious beliefs, their affinity to nature, and appreciation for the Earth. The pow wow began as a harvest celebration. Today, it lures Mesquakies from all over the country back to Iowa to participate in traditional dances and rituals. The Tama County Historical Museum, 200 North Broadway in nearby Toledo, features two floors of Native American artifacts, pioneer items, and a genealogical library.

Otherwise, continue south on State 14. After you cross US 30, follow the signs to Haverhill, ten miles south of Marshalltown. In a frame building just off Main Street, the Matthew Edel Blacksmith Shop remains as it was operated in 1940 when Edel died. Edel immigrated from Germany and settled in Haverhill in 1880. He worked in the shop making horse shoes, hinges, tools, and iron crosses for grave markers until he died. The unpainted wooden walls of the shop are covered with shelves and hangers holding more than 10,000 items including drill bits, tools, templates and scraps of material. With a resurgence in interest in blacksmithing, the shop draws craftspeople as well as historians, and as one state official said, "Here, we are saving the vestiges of an ordinary person's life, not just places associated with a famous or wealthy person." Continue south on State 14 to Newton, just north of I-80.

Newton's claim to fame is that it is the home of the Maytag Corporation, which interestingly enough started out as a manufacturer of farm machinery. But as one local man explained, "Farm machinery was seasonal. As patents ran out, they got on the bandwagon and decided to build a better washing machine. And they did." Maytag didn't leave farming altogether; visitors can still buy blue cheese and other cheese from the Maytag Dairy Farms and watch a video on the making of cheese.

You can learn more about Maytag at the Jasper County Historical Museum, 1700 South Fifteenth Avenue West, just off State 14. The Washing Machine Exhibit is one of the most unusual aspects of the museum. Some seventy-five washing machines are displayed, and all were made by one of nine Newton washing machine companies between 1893 and the present. A Maytag display is part of this exhibit. Another unique part of the museum is a thirty-eight-foot semicircular diorama illustrating in three dimensions the history of the area, starting with the Woodland Indians through 1988. The diorama concludes with a painting of what life is expected to be like a hundred years from now. The two-story 18,400-square-foot building includes a Victorian home, country school, country church, 1910 general store, 1930s home, early barbershop, blacksmith shop, and an agricultural area

115

that includes information on the Jasper County farmer who designed the first Farmall tractor, later manufactured by McCormick in 1924. An identical model made in 1929 is on display. An 1875 barn, moved from a century farm (one that has been owned by one family for at least a hundred years), is displayed outside.

Newton also is home to La Corsette, a gourmet restaurant in a turn-of-the-century mission-style mansion, where tuxedoed waiters serve you before a crackling fireplace, and a pianist entertains on the baby grand piano. Owner Kay Owen started her dream career as a Dayton (Iowa) farm girl who loved to cook. She taught school and bred quarter horses before opening a gourmet restaurant in her farmhouse. The house was built by August Bergman, a state senator, in 1909. She fell in love with the Newton mansion, bought it, and moved, eventually turning four bedrooms into La Corsette Maison, a bed and breakfast. The 5,200-square-foot, twenty-one-room house features beveled and leaded glass, stunning woodwork, and brass fixtures. Take State 14 south and State 163 southeast to Pella.

In the spring of 1847, four ships with 800 Hollanders came to Baltimore, Maryland. They were met by Dominie (pastor) Henry Peter Scholte, the leader who took them to Marion County, Iowa. There, they bought 18,000 acres for $1.25 per acre, and by August 1847 they made cabins or sod houses with thatched roofs. Eventually, they founded Pella, "City of Refuge," where they enjoyed religious freedom, in contrast to Holland where the government controlled the churches. The winter of 1848–49, they lost nearly all their livestock, but new immigrants came with new enthusiasm, seeds, and money. As a result of community strength, Pella prospered, and by 1870 the population had grown to 2,000. That same year, high land prices drove Henry Hospers and some sixty-five families to northwest Iowa where they founded Orange City. The Dutch introduced vegetable and flower gardens, transplanting wild strawberries, roses, lilies, and peach and plum trees, and planting seeds they brought from Holland. They planted flax, which could be spun and woven into linen. These colorful and well-tended gardens earned Pella the name the Garden City. In 1936 the town established the annual Tulip Festival, which garnered national attention.

Pella is one of the cleanest, neatest towns you will see. You are hard-pressed to find a house with peeling paint, a sagging porch, or a garden overrun with weeds. Nary a rusty car sitting on cement blocks. Instead, homes and lawns are immaculate, and colorful flower gardens abound. In the 1960s the residents of Pella had the foresight to restore and enhance the Dutch image of the downtown area. Buildings from the 1800s to early 1900s, ranging from plain but nice to elaborate, face a city park that is a riot of blooming color in spring and summer.

State 163 becomes Washington Street in Pella. On your right, the Strawtown buildings, 1100 block, are some of the oldest in town. The Country Store was built in 1854 to house Central College. The store features Dutch Lace, delftware, children's books, floral arrangements, and Christmas decorations. The Strawtown Inn, a seventeen-room inn, features a dining room with a strong reputation for Dutch and gourmet fare. The restaurant includes a rustic cellar bar and grill and charming dining rooms graced with filmy, lace curtains and sparkling chandeliers. Both are named for the thatched roofs early pioneers used on their sod houses.

Farther down, at 812 Washington Street, is the Red Ribbon Antique Mall. The shop, which was in the house built in the 1850s, was the Red Ribbon Cigar Company in the early 1900s; there's a display of cigars and tobacco-related paraphernalia. A Dutch barn added to the rear of the house provides

117

Visit the Red Ribbon Antique Mall with two stories of antiques

two stories of display space for antiques. In the loft is a coffee shop with Dutch pastries. Continue on Washington Street into the town square. Just north of the square at 728 Washington Street, is the Scholte House, built by Dominie Scholte, head of the early Dutch settlers. In the rear, the gardens include nearly 30,000 flowers. Turn left and go to 820 Main Street. In't Veld Meat Market sells homemade meat products made from old Dutch recipes using hickory smoking and home curing. Try their ring bologna, dried beef, or bratwurst.

Franklin Street, on the far side of the square, is my favorite and a good place to begin a walking tour. On the corner of Main and Franklin Streets is Vande Lune Fabrics, with an exceptional line of fashion and decorator fabrics, quilting and craft fabrics, and classes. When they say mail orders are welcome, they're not kidding; after buying a lovely piece of floral challis to make a skirt, I wanted more for a blouse. Over the phone, I described the fabric and a few days later, it was delivered. Down the street are the town's luscious bakeries, Jaarsma Bakery and Vander Ploegs. The third generation is baking at Jaarsma Bakery, turning out special pastries, such as Dutch letters, St. Nick cookies, and apple bread. Unfortunately, the bakeries don't have seating areas, but in good weather, the square is a great place to enjoy the blooms and pastries.

East of the square on Franklin Street is the Ben Franklin store, with a great collection of craft supplies, fabrics, and souvenirs. A couple of doors away, the Klokkenspel portrays a unique story through the animated figures that are set in motion by the clock at 11:00 A.M., 1:00 P.M., 3:00, 5:00, and 9:00 P.M. On the street side, visitors are entertained with figures telling Pella's history. Pass through the arches into a brick courtyard with six tiled murals and circular benches surrounding flower beds. On the courtyard side, the Klokkenspiel displays Tulip Time figures. The characters move to the music of a 147-bell carillon. Five bronze bells, cast in Holland, toll the hour and play the Westminster chimes. In the same block is the Pella Opera House built in 1900. The three-story brick building has been renovated and hosts a variety of musical and theatrical performances.

Farther down the street is one of the town's top attractions, the Pella Historical Village, surrounding a courtyard and beds with more than 15,000 tulips. The Historical Village includes the Wyatt Earp House, restored to the 1850s period. Wyatt Earp is one of the town's more famous residents. He came to Pella in 1850 at age two with his family. The Earps lived in Pella until Wyatt was fourteen, when his father led a wagon train west to California. The Van Spanckeren Store features antiques from the early settlers including vintage clothing and herbal medicines. Other buildings in the village are a replica of Dominie Scholte's last Pella church; Beason Blommers Grist Mill where you can see corn being ground during festival time; a pottery shop; Klompenshop, featuring Dutch imports and wooden shoes; a Dutch house displaying a collection of dolls dressed in traditional Dutch costumes and a fine collection of Delft; a Dutch bakery that, at festival time, serves coffee and Dutch pastries; and a log cabin that was lived in until 1936. One of the buildings commemorates the Tulip Festivals, held the second full weekend in May, with memorabilia from past events. The festival includes a parade, garden tours, flower arranging competition, stage performances, concerts, Dutch dance performances, street scrubbing, and church worship services.

Just south of the town square is the Fire Station Museum, displaying antique fire fighting equipment and memorabilia. Farther south, at Main and Oskaloosa Streets, is the old Pella train depot, now the Rolscreen Museum, which features exhibits about the Pella Corporation.

In the Area

Phone ahead as several attractions are open only seasonally.

Briar Patch Tea Room (Conrad): 515-366-2228

Conrad General Store (Conrad): 515-366-2043

Marlyne's Palletable Gifts (Conrad): 515-366-2032

Watson's Grocery Store (State Center): 515-483-2458

Tama County Historical Museum (Toledo): 515-484-6767

Matthew Edel Blacksmith Shop (Haverhill): 515-475-3299

Newton Convention and Tourism Bureau (Newton):
515-792-0299 or 800-798-0299

Jasper County Historical Museum (Newton): 515-792-9118

La Corsette Maison Bed and Breakfast (Newton):
515-792-6833

Pella Chamber of Commerce (Pella): 515-628-4311

Pella Historical Village (Pella): 515-628-2409

Strawtown Country Store (Pella): 515-628-4004

Scholte House (Pella): 515-628-3684

In't Veld Meat Market (Pella): 515-628-3440

Vande Lune Fabrics (Pella): 515-628-3350

Jaarsma Bakery (Pella): 515-628-2940

Vander Ploegs Bakery (Pella): 515-628-2293

Pella Opera House (Pella): 515-628-8628 or 628-8625

9 ~

Central Iowa— Railroads, Historical Farms, and Covered Bridges

From Des Moines: Take I-235 north to Ames.

Highlights: *Farm House Museum, Iowa State University, Boone and Scenic Valley Railroad, Iowa Arboretum, Kate Shelley Memorial Park and Railroad Museum, Mamie Doud Eisenhower Birthplace, Living History Farms, State Capitol Building, Sherman Hill Historic District, historic covered bridges, John Wayne Birthplace. Take two to three days for this trip.*

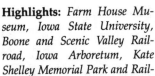

While the lives of most prairie settlers were plain and ordinary and filled with a lot of hard work, the valiant, the famous, the rags-to-riches life stories offer us inspiration and promise. These are some of those stories. The heroism of a young woman who risked her life to save the lives of unknown passengers on an oncoming train; a baby born in Boone, Iowa, who would one day marry a man destined to become president of the United States; an Irish immigrant who worked his way to becoming a wealthy farmer; turn-of-the-century developers; the son of common Winterset folks who grew up to be a star of the silver screen. These, then, are some of the stories of central Iowa.

In Ames, the Farm House Museum, the first building on the Iowa State University campus, first housed university farm superintendents and later the deans. Constructed in 1860 of native brick, it has been restored and furnished in the period 1869–1910. Iowa State University is the state's land grant university, opening in 1869. The campus for some 25,000 students includes several historic buildings and several Christian Petersen sculptures and Grant Wood murals. The Brunnier Gallery and Museum in the Scheman Building at the ISU Center is a decorative arts museum with a national reputation. The museum is devoted to historic and contemporary fine arts. It features ceramics, pottery, porcelain, glass, enameling, jade, ivory, and a large collection of dolls. Travel west on US 30 to Boone.

Boone County was named for Capt. Nathan Boone of the U.S. Dragoons, the youngest son of pioneer Daniel Boone. Captain Boone was part of an expedition that started marching in 1835 from Old Fort Des Moines to the village of the great Sioux chief, Wabasha, now Winona, Minnesota. The Iowa settlement was first called Montana, but its name was changed to Boone in 1871. In Boone, go west on Story Street and west on Tenth or Eleventh Streets six blocks to the depot for the Boone and Scenic Valley Railroad.

"Did any of you kids bring along your bungee cords?" the conductor asked as the train chugged across the Bass Point Creek Bridge, 800 feet long and 156 feet in the air. Autumn is the best time to travel this scenic fourteen-mile trip through the wooded Des Moines River Valley to Fraser, a ghost of a one-time rip-roaring mining town. The train passed summer blooms of honeysuckle and purple phlox. The Iowan, which runs only on weekends and holidays, is the line's Chinese steam locomotive, the first Chinese locomotive imported to the United States and the only one of its class in the country. The day we rode the train, the elegant red and black locomotive was down for overhaul. Along the way, you can see the Kate Shelley Bridge, six miles southwest. At 185 feet high, it's one of—if not THE—highest double-track bridges in the world, according to the conductor. (More on the courageous Kate Shelley below.) The B&SV depot complex includes an Iowa railroad museum, railroad equipment, trolley rides, gift shop, and snack bar. After you take the train ride, drive west on State 30 and north on County P70 six miles north of Ogden to visit the Hickory Grove Country School Museum in the Don Williams Recreation Area. The one-room school was built in 1889 and served Yell Township until 1956. It contains authentic clothing worn by teachers and students, original double desks, pot-bellied stove, pump organ, textbooks, and a video presentation on rural schools in the county.

Back in Boone, two blocks south of the B&SV station is the birthplace of Mamie Doud Eisenhower and her home for the first six months of her life. This one-story yellow frame house has been completely restored and contains many pieces of furniture from the Doud family, including the bed in which Mamie was born in 1896. Mrs. Eisenhower visited the home several times, I was told by the middle-aged woman who was my guide. Mrs. Eisenhower personally brought two chairs to the home. "She always came by limousine," said the guide. "So I imagine she just put them in the back of that limo and said 'We're goin' ta Boone.'" A basement library displays memorabilia from the Eisenhower years, including a sketch by Elizabeth Arden of Mamie's hair and styling instructions so that local hairdressers could maintain the "Mamie look" when the First Lady traveled.

Four blocks southwest is the Boone County Cultural Center and Historical Museum. Housed in an eighty-five-year-old former Masonic Temple and listed on the National Register of

Boone & Scenic Valley Railroad

Historic Places, the museum tells the story of Boone County from prehistoric times to the present. Three blocks north, the Boone County Museum, a private enterprise, includes artifacts, 100-year-old Indian ceremonial dress, replica of an Indian longhouse, cast-iron bank collection, antique toys, tools, early advertising, and postcards. Head south of Boone on State 164, west on US 30, and south on County R18 to Moingona.

Five miles southwest of Boone is the Kate Shelley Memorial Park and Railroad Museum, memorializing a teenage heroine. In 1881 Kate Shelley, fifteen, braved a terrible storm by crawling across a railroad bridge to warn the depot and oncoming passenger train of a washed-out bridge at the site. The depot exhibit includes a ticket window, telegraph, hand-cranked wall telephone, and variety of railroad memorabilia. Backtrack to US 30 and head east, then take State 164 south.

In Ledges State Park, sandstone rock formations twenty-five to seventy-five feet high once drew Native Americans for their councils and pow wows. Today, motorists can see the Ledges from the winding road and you can hike to several areas with views of the Des Moines River and valley. Some of the state's largest maple, cottonwood, and ash trees are found in this 1,200-acre park. Head east on County E57, turn south on a gravel road and follow the signs to the Iowa Arboretum, which includes more than 300 acres of woods, meadows, and walking trails, a forty-acre "Library of Living Plants" with trees, hosta gardens, roses, peonies, and other shrubs and flowers. Continue east on County E57, head south on State 17, which becomes State 141 and I-35, then take I-80 east, exiting at Merle Hay Road. Continue north .25 mile on Merle Hay Road to Heard Gardens.

Heard Gardens is one of the country's leading suppliers of mail order lilacs, and you can visit their retail gardens in Johnston. The business was established in 1928 by Clyde Heard (he even has a lilac variety named after him) and now is owned by Bob and Mary Anne Rennebohm. The company ships lilacs around the world and has supplied several for the White House gardens. Backtrack to I-80 heading west, take the Hickman Road exit to the Living History Farms.

The Living History Farms is a 600-acre open-air agricultural museum featuring buildings, planting methods, and livestock authentic to the periods represented. We started in the 1875 village of Walnut Hill with a blacksmith shop, mercantile, broommaker, church, and the opulent farmhouse, the historic Flynn Mansion. We were fascinated watching a broommaker. "The broom shop is based on an Indianola broom factory in the 1870s," he said. At that time, there were 2,300 acres in the state planted to broomcord, a sorghum plant that grew five to fifteen feet tall. The tassels were used for making brooms. Later, in the gift shop, my daughter HAD to have her very own junior-sized broom. Consumer note: parents, these brooms are great investments and educational tools; my daughter now loves to sweep the kitchen and the garage. The gift shop also has an excellent collection of books on Iowa.

Tractor-drawn carts take you on a walking time line of 300 years of Iowa agriculture, first a 1700 Ioway Indian village, pioneer farm from 1850, horse farm of 1900, and the Henry A. Wallace crop center with exhibits on modern agriculture. Along the way, interpreters in period costume recreate daily routines on the farm. The Flynn mansion was built in the 1860s by Martin Flynn, who immigrated from Ireland at age twelve and worked his way up in the railroad to running his own 1,200-acre shorthorn cattle farm. Tourists should be aware that Flynn was exceptional—most Iowa farmhouses are a far cry from the opulence found in this mansion.

Take I-235 east into Des Moines, going south on Forty-second Street and east on John Lynde Road to Salisbury House located on eleven acres of woods in the middle of the city. This forty-two-room English Tudor mansion is a replica of

King's House in Salisbury, England. It includes authentic Tudor furnishings and contains art from around the world. It is owned and maintained by the Iowa Educational Association.

Continue east on I-235 to the State Historical Building, Grand Avenue and East Sixth Street, with numerous hands-on historical exhibits and an Iowa gift shop. Just east of there the 275-foot gold-leaf dome and four smaller domes atop the Iowa Capitol Building gleam in the dawn and the setting sun. The grounds include gardens, sculptures, and monuments. Inside, there are legislative and court chambers, the governor's office, a law library, numerous artworks, a grand staircase, a scale model of the battleship *Iowa*, and a collection of First Lady dolls. Tours are available. Go a block south to Court Avenue and head west to what is now called the Administrative Office Building, 111 Court Avenue. The building was once the Des Moines post office, a beaux-arts classical-style structure built in 1908 and is on the National Register of Historic Places. In the north lobby of this building is the Polk County Heritage Gallery.

Head west on Walnut Street, north on Tenth Street and west on Woodland Avenue, to the Sherman Hill Historic District, a thirty-block neighborhood of Victorian homes under renovation by their owners. Sophisticated apartments, mansions, and simple cottages from the Victorian era and the turn of the century are in several stages of restoration. The area extends to Fifteenth Street on the east, High Street on the south, I-235 on the north, and Woodland Cemetery on the west. This area developed in the 1870s when Hoyt Sherman, then postmaster, bought a five-acre tract and built a Gothic-style cottage. Sherman became president of a large insurance company, and with his rise in social status, he transformed the once modest cottage into an opulent Italianate mansion. Today, Hoyt Sherman Place is open to the public by reservation. It features carved woodwork, wainscotting, marble fireplaces, and brass chandeliers, and is elegantly furnished with period pieces. Other well-known Iowans, including Henry Wallace, founder of Wallace's *Farmer,* and Aaron Younker of Younkers Department Stores, lived there. In the early 1900s, luxury apartment buildings appeared in the neighborhood. The Crowell, 669 Seventeenth Street, a Flemish Renaissance Revival structure, was built in 1905 with four spacious apartments with fireplaces, built-in buffets, and beamed ceilings. The Lexington, 1721 Pleasant Street, built in 1908, boasted having the first "boyless" elevator west of the Mississippi; it still has the original brass elevator. Each year in September the neighborhood association sponsors a fundraiser in which the public can see the interiors of some of the homes. Head south to Grand Avenue and take it west for the next grand home.

Terrace Hill, 2300 Grand Avenue, a restored 1869 Victorian mansion, is an outstanding example of elaborate Second Empire architecture. The governor's official residence is on the third floor. Tours of the first two floors and carriage house museum are available. Continue west on Grand Avenue to West Des Moines. Head south (left) on Fifth Street.

West Des Moines was once a railroad town, and Historic Valley Junction, in the 100-300 blocks of Fifth Street, has been restored and renovated. It's easy to while away half a day in the antique shops, boutiques, and specialty shops here. In the summer, there is a farmer's market. Continue south on Fifth Street, turn right (west) on Railroad Avenue, passing the fire station. Take Grand Avenue southwest and turn right or west onto Fuller Road. You will go through an industrial park, but don't give up hope. At 2001 Fuller Road, you will come to the historic Jordan House. The first white settler in Walnut township lived in this sixteen-room 1850s home, which was later a stop on the Underground Railroad. Rooms have been restored from the 1850s and 1880s. To reach I-35, take Fuller Road west, go south (left) on South Thirty-fifth Street and southwest (right) on Grand Avenue. Take I-35 south. For a look at some of the more unusual crops in Iowa, take exit 65 to Cumming for a look at the Howell Tree Farm, where three families live with 40,000 Christmas trees and ten acres of flowers for dried arrangements. Take County G14 three miles west and County G4R 1.25 miles south, following the signs. Backtrack to I-35 and continue south. Although you are traveling on an interstate, this country road passes through gentle rolling hills, stands of oak and hickory, and gives motorists glimpses of farms.

You can start the covered bridges tour by leaving I-35 at exit 52 and heading west on County G50 to St. Charles. If you want to go straight to Winterset, take exit 56 onto State 92 west.

In the fall, the wooded, rolling hills around Winterset, originally a Quaker settlement, are ablaze with color. The covered bridges have existed for more than 100 years, but they reached national prominence in the book, *The Bridges of Madison County*, by Robert Waller. If you don't have time to visit all six covered bridges, you can see the Cutler-Donahoe Bridge in the Winterset City Park. The bridge, built in 1871, originally crossed the North River near Bevington. It is open to foot traffic only.

The six covered bridges, all listed on the National Register of Historic Places, are within twelve miles of Winterset. For the bridge tour, start in St. Charles, southeast of Winterset. The Imes Bridge, built in 1870, first crossed the Middle River near Patterson. In 1887 it was moved to Clanton Creek, southwest of St. Charles, where it was used until 1977. It now sits in a park on the east side of St. Charles. Head west on County G50 to the Holliwell Bridge, three miles southeast of Winterset. The Holliwell Bridge spans the Middle River on what was once the main highway of earlier Madison County. Continue on County G50 into Winterset to see the Cutler-Donahoe Bridge in the city park. Go through town and head east on State 92 and follow the signs to the Cedar Bridge

130

northeast of town. Built in 1883, it spanned Cedar Creek on what is now State 169. The Cedar Bridge was moved to its present location in 1920. Backtrack into town and take State 169 north and follow the signs to the Hogback Bridge, five miles northwest of Winterset. This bridge is at its original site spanning the North River. Built in 1880 it features a 100-foot span, the longest of the covered bridges in the county. Backtrack to State 92 and head west. Follow the signs to the Roseman Bridge, featured in Waller's book, southwest of town. It spans the Middle River five miles west of Pammel State Park. On our way to the Roseman Bridge, the winding gravel road took us past a quiet stream. Queen Anne's lace bobbed in the summer breeze while a mother pheasant and her young scuttled along in the dust. "Baby birds, Mom, baby birds," my daughter announced. "Say that to your tape recorder."

The Madison County Courthouse square is the center for the Covered Bridge Festival, held the second full weekend in October. The building, crafted of native limestone, features a solid walnut staircase. The old-fashioned dome is a local landmark. Just a few blocks southeast of the courthouse at 224 South Second Street is a four-room, white frame house where John Wayne was born Marion Robert Morrison on May 26, 1907. The cottage has been restored to the early 1900s period and it features memorabilia from Wayne's career as a gunslinging movie star. An Iowa Welcome Center is adjacent to the cottage.

On the south side of town at 815 South Second Avenue is the Madison County Historical Complex, eighteen acres of living history lovingly restored by Madison County volunteers. The restored 1856 Bevington-Kaser buildings, a brick mansion, stone barn, and privy are the nucleus of the complex. The barn and privy are built of limestone from owner C. D. "Doc" Bevington's quarry south of Winterset. Bricks were fired in his kiln, and wood for the verandas, window casings, and gingerbread trim was harvested from his land.

Other structures moved onto the site include a log cabin school, log post office, the Field Mercantile, Winterset train depot, blacksmith shop, and 1881 Zion Church. The museum contains a large fossil and mineral collection and personal letters and memorabilia of George Washington Carver.

Winterset's history includes a generous humanitarian spirit, first engendered by the original Quaker settlers. The painted brick house, now the Winterset Art Center, built in about 1854, was once a station on the Underground Railroad. The town pays tribute to famous resident George Washington Carver with a niche in the art center and a park dedicated in his name. The park is on East Court Avenue between the fire station and Brittain's Furniture Store. Carver arrived in town having been refused entrance to a college in another state after officials saw that he was black. In Winterset, where he was treated with kindness, he found encouragement to rise above the prejudice, ignorance, and poverty he had experienced. He went on to attend Simpson College in Indianola and Iowa State University in Ames, where he became a respected faculty member. Carver befriended another nationally known Winterset resident, Henry A. Wallace, plant scientist, founder of Pioneer Hybrid International Company, U.S. secretary of agriculture, and vice president of the United States. He was the grandson of Henry Wallace, publisher and editor of the *Winterset Madisonian* from 1878–88.

In the Area

Phone ahead as several attractions are open only seasonally.

Ames Convention and Tourism Bureau (Ames):
    515-232-4032 or 800-288-7470

Farm House Museum (Ames): 515-294-3342

Iowa State University (Ames): 515-294-4777

Brunnier Gallery and Museum (Ames): 515-294-3342

Boone and Scenic Valley Railroad (Boone): 515-432-4249 or 800-626-0319

Mamie Doud Eisenhower Birthplace (Boone): 515-432-1896

Boone County Cultural Center and Historical Museum (Boone): 515-432-1907

Boone County Museum (Boone): 515-432-1730

Kate Shelley Memorial Park and Railroad Museum (Moingona): 515-432-3342

Iowa Arboretum (Madrid): 515-795-3216

Des Moines Convention and Tourism Bureau (Des Moines): 515-286-4960 or 800-451-2625

Heard Gardens (Johnston): 515-276-4533

Living History Farms (Des Moines): 515-278-5286

Salisbury House (Des Moines): 515-279-9711

Sherman Hill Historic District (Des Moines): 515-284-5717

State Historical Building (Des Moines): 515-281-5111

State Capitol Building (Des Moines): 515-281-5591

Polk County Heritage Gallery (Des Moines): 515-286-3215

Hoyt Sherman Place (Des Moines): 515-243-0913

Terrace Hill (Des Moines): 515-281-3604

Historic Valley Junction (West Des Moines): 515-223-3286

Jordan House (West Des Moines): 515-225-1286

Howell Tree Farm (Cumming): 515-981-0863

Historic Covered Bridges (Winterset): 515-462-1185

John Wayne Birthplace (Winterset): 515-462-1044

Madison County Historical Complex (Winterset): 515-462-2134

10 ~

South-central Iowa to the Loess Hills

From Des Moines: Take I-35 south to exit 33 and head west on US 34 to Creston.

From Council Bluffs: Take US 275 south to Glenwood and reverse the order of this trip.

Highlights: *Creston Restored Depot, Union County Historical Museum Complex, Red Oak Heritage Hill, Swedish town of Stanton, Greater Shenandoah Historical Center, Nodaway Valley Historical Museum in Clarinda, Fremont County Historical Museum Complex in Sidney, loess hills bluffs. Allow at least two days for the entire trip.*

This trip takes you from the generally flat land of south-central Iowa to the rolling hills, bluffs, and ravines of western Iowa's loess hills. Along the way, we visit old railroad communities and a utopian society, cross the Mormon Trail, and traverse part of the Dragoon Trail. The loess hills run parallel to the Missouri River from Akron, north of Sioux City, to the Iowa-Missouri border. We will view them in southwestern Iowa around Sidney, Riverton, and Glenwood. These rolling hills are the product of thousands of years of activity creating a geological wonder found only here and in China. Glacial movement ground rock below it into a fine powder, which

Glenwood's loess hills

was carried down rivers during summer glacial melt. In winter when the water movement slowed or stopped, silt was deposited in the floodplains. Later, wind blew the silt and deposited it in drifts as high as 200 feet along the eastern edge of the floodplain. This process, repeated over thousands of years, created the loess hills. More recently, erosion has formed deep ravines prevalent in the hills today. The hills provide habitat for butterflies, birds, mammals, reptiles, and amphibians. Although much of Iowa has been plowed into cropland, the hills remain predominantly covered with prairie and woods. Desertlike microclimates have formed in some of the well-drained steep ridges exposed to harsh sun and winds. As such, the loess hills are a focus of scientific research and educational and conservation efforts.

"Generations of people remembered Mitchell Rice when they got off the train in Creston," said museum director Jane Briley. "He'd be there with his shoe shine stand ready to do their shoes." Today, Rice's shoe shine stand, housed in the Union County Historical Museum Complex at McKinley Park, is just one of several things that evoke memories of Creston's history as a railroad town. Throughout the town you can see impressive Victorian homes, built at a time when the railroad made the town a bustling center of business activity.

The restored Creston Depot on Adams Street is another reminder of the town's railroad heritage. Enter the waiting room, and you'll feel transported back in history to the time when marble floors, tiled columns, and wooden benches were customary. Now city offices are also in the restored depot. To the east are the remains of one of the world's largest roundhouses, a bridgelike structure that the railroad still uses. At one time the town was home to 1,800 railroad employees. Nearby is the Creston Power Plant Antique Mall in an old brick power plant.

At the McKinley Park complex, you can see more rail-road equipment—the caboose, an old depot, and the signal tower in the re-creation of an 1890s town. This illustrates the self-sufficiency of these little towns, which provided a post office, supplies, market, and access to a train. The day I visited, Briley left an informal meeting in the Spaulding 1878 Methodist Church to show me around. My daughter Elizabeth, five, and nephew Adam, nine, liked Lake McKinley. While I toured the village, my sister watched them delighting themselves by throwing rocks in the water.

In addition to the railroad items, original buildings include Lincoln No. 5 School, the last operating country school in the county. "Marcella (Howe) here," Briley introduced her to me, "was a teacher in that school. Children in first through eighth grades went there until it closed in 1966." Marcella smiled, "We still have the recitation bench where the children recited their lessons." The school contains all sorts of memorabilia including an early map of Iowa showing locations of the various groups of Indians. The museum also contains an 1855 log cabin, an 1896 barn and replicas of a general store, blacksmith shop, barber shop, harness shop, fire station, machine shed that exhibits a collection of original horsedrawn machinery, and a grist mill. A museum contains vintage clothing, quilts, furniture, a collection of barbed wire, and more. The third weekend in September, Creston hosts the Annual Southwest Iowa Professional Hot Air Balloon Races. Continue west on US 34 to Corning.

A movement toward a perfect society lived out its existence three miles east of Corning in the last half of the 1800s. The Icarian Colony is part of Adams County history. Of several social movements emanating from Central Europe from 1850 to 1900, the Icarian Colony was the longest existing, nonreligious communal experiment in America. Frenchman Etienne Cabet, who published a book on his ideas of "Utopia," led some 400 Europeans to Nauvoo, Illinois, after the Mormons left, and eventually Cabet and eighty followers came to Corning. Cabet died in 1856 before Icaria was incorporated as an agricultural society in 1860. Cabet's principles lived on through the community until it gave way to restlessness and the thrust of individualism, and by 1898 it had dissolved. The Icarians are credited with introducing grapes, rhubarb, asparagus, and lilacs to the area. The town still has an occasional rhubarb pie feed, celebrating just one of the fruits of the Icarians' labor.

The Icarian school was moved to the west side of Corning for restoration and display. Furnishings include school desks made from native lumber and the first ones used in the county, pot-bellied stove, recitation bench, and other pieces common in one-room schoolhouses during the 1800s. The Adams County House of History, at Tenth and Benton Streets, the county jail for about eighty years, is a mosaic of donations from county residents. The main floor includes antique furniture, china, glass, and silver. Criminals were kept in jail cells in the cellar. On the other side of the bars is the original dining room and kitchen that the sheriff and his family used in 1877. The second floor features historical literature and archives, and a room exhibiting Icarian memorabilia. Lake Icaria, four miles north of Corning, offers a variety of water activities, including boat rentals, water ski zone, excellent fishing, a 300-foot beach, and a motion-impaired pier making the lake and a fish cleaning station accessible to people in wheelchairs. Although not related, Corning can add two more points to its fame: it is the birthplace of Johnny Carson and headquarters for the National Farmers Organization, a grass roots organization founded in the 1950s. Continue west on US 34, taking a jog south on County M63 into the little town of Stanton.

Stanton is a small community founded by Swedish immigrants, a notion well illustrated with the town water tower that has been transformed into a giant Swedish coffee pot.

The town's heritage is evident in its festivals, foods, and Swedish signs for many businesses. "Mrs. Olson" on the Folgers coffee commercials is a Stanton daughter, Virginia Christine. Swedes founded the town in 1870 along the Burlington Northern Railroad and US 34. The town looks especially well scrubbed with its rows of white houses and well-trimmed lawns. The Mamrelund Lutheran Church, also founded by Swedish immigrants, is a Gothic stone structure with beautiful stained glass windows. The Old Main elementary school building is Montgomery County's oldest public building. For Scandinavian gifts and bakery items, try the Troll House at 313 Broad Avenue. Backtrack to US 34 and continue west.

The first white settlers came to Red Oak in the 1850s. When the railroad arrived in 1869, a flurry of building took place, and the county tripled in size with Red Oak as the economic hub. The Heritage Hill walking tour focuses on the elaborate architecture of eighteen residences and public buildings. The tour includes the Montgomery County Courthouse, built in 1890 of Missouri limestone, featuring Gothic Revival architecture. The interior features wrought iron, marble, stained glass, and original tile. A line drawing of the courthouse used on a wall calendar led to the development of the Thos. D. Murphy Company, the town's oldest business. Theater, comedy, even crafts were part of the summer entertainment appearing at the Chautauqua Pavilion for twenty years. The landmark has been restored and is on the National Register of Historic Places. Brochures detailing a walking tour of Heritage Hill are available from the Chamber of Commerce, 405 Reed Street. Head south on State 48 to Shenandoah.

Shenandoah's roots go back to radio, the gardening and nursery business, and Mormonism. The settlement of Manti, an 1850s Mormon community, eventually became the town of Shenandoah. The Greater Shenandoah Historical Center at 304 Sheridan Avenue tells the story of Mormon migration and the religious group's ties with the town, as well as the story of the development of radio there. Two well-known gardening names hail from Shenandoah. Henry Field started his seed and nursery business there, and Earl May, who married into a family in the nursery business, started a seed company, too. Competition grew and each started a radio station to advertise his products. The stations, KMA and KFNF, at one time were the most powerful in the state. Head south through town and on State 2 west to the Earl May Show Gardens, where you will find twenty-five acres of flowers, vegetables, grasses, trees, roses, perennial gardens, and trails. Two other famous Shenandoans are the Everly brothers, whose "parents were entertainers—they sang hillbilly music, uh, bluegrass, before country was 'in,'" said a local woman. The Everly brothers (of "Wake Up, Little Susie" fame) performed on Radio KMA while they lived in Shenandoah. The city has erected a monument to the singing brothers at the Depot Deli on Sheridan Avenue.

You can pick up the Wabash Trace Nature Trail in Shenandoah. Started in 1988, the Wabash Trace is a rails-to-trails project converting railroad right-of-ways to recreational areas. The sixty-three-mile-long nature trail open for walking, hiking, bicycling, and cross-country skiing cuts diagonally across Fremont County starting in Blanchard in the southeast and going through Imogene and Malvern, then into Silver City and Council Bluffs. The prairie grasses along the southern end of the trail fed herds of buffalo and deer that once roamed the area. The original Wabash Depot in Shenandoah has been preserved. Some of the service depots that provided homesteaders with their essentials grew into settlements and towns, others faded away.

Head east on State 2 to Clarinda, a stop on the Underground Railway and birthplace of Glenn Miller. Named after a pioneer's niece, Clarinda, platted in 1853, sits among rolling hills and prairie lands of the Nodaway River Valley. Glenn

Miller, trombonist and big band leader, was born in Clarinda, March 1, 1904, at the now restored home, 601 South Glenn Miller Avenue, between the museum and the town square. Glenn Miller organized his own band in 1936 and was the first musician in America to receive a Gold Record—for the song "Chattanooga Choo Choo." The town's annual Glenn Miller festival is held in June. The Nodaway Valley Historical Museum features displays on Miller, the clock and bell that rang in the Clarinda South School in 1875, as well as artifacts from the origins of the 4-H Club. The Goldenrod School, now on the Page County Fairgrounds, is where Jessie Shambaugh, one of the founders of the international 4-H movement, taught in the early 1900s. In her after-school groups, she taught her students skills that related directly to farm life, such "home arts" for the girls and corn germination testing techniques to the boys. "Is that like genetic engineering?" jeered one high school–aged boy dressed in baggy shorts, T-shirt, athletic shoes, and baseball cap worn backward. He was traveling with his family. "Well, just look what random selection gives us," muttered his father under his breath. Ms. Shambaugh eventually developed the Boys' Corn Clubs and Girls' Home Clubs, and designed the 4-H pin.

In the 1880s Clarinda was named the site for the State Hospital for the Insane (now the Clarinda Treatment Center), and now a museum, the Clarinda Mental Health Institution Museum, 1800 North Sixteenth Street, exhibits tools, furnishings, and items from mental health care from the 1800s. "This looks like torture," exclaimed a teenage girl with braces and headphones who was touring the museum. "Well, there was a lot of weird stuff going on in those days," advised her boyfriend. Backtrack on State 2 west of Shenandoah.

The Pleasant Overview Loop, encompassing about twenty miles in the loess hills area, takes you through the spring and fall flyway for thousands of migrating geese and ducks who take refuge, along with bald eagles, in the

Riverton Wildlife Refuge. The route starts at the intersection of State 2 and County L68. Take State 2 west to Sidney, County J34 farther west, south on County L44 (where you can take a three-mile Spring Valley Loop). Take County J46 east to US 275. Just south of that intersection is Waubonsie State Park, an excellent example of remaining upland forests and prairies of the loess hills. Finish the loop by continuing east on County J46 to Riverton and north on County L68 back to State 2.

The Spring Valley Loop gives visitors a glimpse inside of the loess hills. Once you are going south on County L44, take the first gravel road on your left (heading east) and take another left (heading south). From these gravel roads, you can view steep ravines and high bluffs. You also can see caves or brick-faced cellars, half-hidden in the ground, that were originally incorporated into the homes of early settlers. Back-track to Sidney.

The Fremont County Historical Museum Complex, on the east side of the Sidney town square, features Penn's Drug Store built in 1865 with its soda fountain, a country school-house, Native American artifacts collected around the county, quilt display, and an 1893 Baptist Church. Sidney is the county seat, and the courthouse was built in 1889. The town also is well known for the Sidney Rodeo, starting the second Wednesday in August. Cowboys from all over the country come for calf roping, bull dogging, bronc riding, and bareback competitions. Continue north on US 275 to Tabor.

Entering Tabor from the south, turn left or west on Orange Street. At the northeast corner of Orange and Center Streets is the site of the house of Jonas Jones, friend of abolitionist leader John Brown. Brown often visited Jones, and rumor has it that there was a secret tunnel from this house to the one diagonally across the street. There is little left of the original house except some large timbers. Go another block west and turn right on Park Street to the Todd House Museum, which is open by appointment. Built in 1853 of native black walnut, oak, and cottonwood, this house was one of the stations on the Underground Railroad. The trip ends here, but you can head north to Council Bluffs and Missouri Valley for the west central Iowa route.

In the Area

Phone ahead as several attractions are open only seasonally.

Union County Historical Museum (Creston): 515-782-4525

Restored Creston Depot (Creston): 515-782-7021

Lake Icaria (Corning): 515-322-4793

Adams County House of History (Corning): 515-322-3241

Heritage Hill Tour (Red Oak): 712-623-4821

Greater Shenandoah Historical Center (Shenandoah): 712-246-1669

Earl May Show Garden (Shenandoah): 712-246-1020

Shenandoah Chamber of Commerce (Shenandoah): 712-246-3260

Nodaway Valley Historical Museum (Clarinda): 712-542-3073

Fremont County Historical Museum Complex (Sidney): 712-374-2719

Todd House (Tabor): 712-629-2675

11 ~
Apple Orchards, Donna Reed, and Prairie Gardens

From Council Bluffs: Take State 183 north to Missouri Valley.

From Des Moines: Take I-80 and I-680 west, and State 183 north to Missouri Valley.

Highlights: *DeSoto Wildlife Refuge, Harrison County Museum, Small's Fruit Farm, White's Floral Garden, Dow House, Donna Reed Festival and Artist Workshops, McHenry House, Prairie Peddler. Allow one to two days for this trip.*

This is the second loess hills route in this book. West-central Iowa contains a variety of natural scenery including farmland, river valleys, gently rolling foothills, and the loess hills. This is the state's apple-growing region. As the little country roads wind around the hills, you will see orchards that produce the fruit for Small's Orchards and other producers. Marked routes include historic trails of Lewis and Clark, early stagecoach roads, apple orchards, and the original Lincoln Highway, now US 30. Farther northeast, we visit the historic Dow House in Dow City. Denison is the former home of Donna Reed and now home to an arts festival honoring the late movie star. Our trip concludes in the country gardens of Prairie Pedlar, with blossoms of statice, rose, and lavender and many examples of rural folk art.

Our route starts near Missouri Valley at the DeSoto National Wildlife Refuge that includes DeSoto Lake, woods, grasslands, ponds, and the Missouri River. This rest stop for migrating ducks and geese is one of several refuges to preserve and restore scarce habitat for migratory birds. Much of the development during the last century and a half—in which land has been cleared and drained, the river has been channeled, and flood control measures have been implemented— has adversely affected wildlife habitat. Other birds found in the refuge include warblers, gulls, and shorebirds, in addition to pheasants, bobwhite quail, red-headed woodpeckers, wood ducks, and bank swallows. Some 120 bald eagles have been counted at one time. A restored sandbar in the reserve now attracts nesting piping plovers and interior least terns, the latter of which have been considered endangered throughout the U.S. The area is populated with white-tailed deer, cottontail rabbits, raccoons, coyotes, opossums, foxes, squirrels, beavers, muskrats, and occasionally a mink. There are twelve miles of paved and gravel roads. A special Fall Auto Tour features numbered stops with an interpretive brochure describing bird migration. The refuge offers several walking and hiking trails, fishing, boating, and mushroom gathering.

It is believed that Lewis and Clark, who visited the area in August 1804 and are believed to have been the first white explorers in the area, camped at a point just below the river loop called DeSoto Bend in or near the refuge. Several decades after Lewis and Clark's expedition, the Missouri River became an important artery for trade among outposts on the frontier, but the river was dangerous with shallow spots and snags. All told, some 400 steamboats sank or were stranded between St. Louis, Missouri, and Fort Benton, Montana.

The *Bertrand* was one of them. In 1968 the *Bertrand* was discovered on the DeSoto Refuge. The 1860s steamboat was a mountain packet stern-wheeler designed to hold more than 250 tons of cargo and to navigate the shallow, narrow western rivers. Today, the *Betrrand* Museum on the refuge contains more than 200,000 artifacts from the boat that was stocked with supplies for the Montana gold rush in 1864. The exhibit offers a glimpse into life at the end of the Civil War. Head north on State 183 to Missouri Valley.

You can't help but notice the Harrison County Museum and Iowa Welcome Center along US 30 near Missouri Valley— a whole village of log buildings stands alongside the highway. Eleven structures include an 1853 log cabin, chapel, and jail, and an 1868 "Iowa Standard Rural School" is preserved as it was when it was closed. The displays also include a peddler's wagon, doctor's office, and Native American artifacts. The Iowa Welcome Center includes an Iowa Products Store stocked with items produced from within the state.

After rambling around the historical village, my sister and I took her son Adam and my daughter Elizabeth on a little walk up the hill to the Apple Orchard Inn Bed and Breakfast. The home features decor from the 1930s including lace curtains and an old-fashioned radio the size of a bookcase. The rural home offers views of the Boyer River Valley and twenty-six acres of loess hills orchards, in addition to walking and hiking trails. Country gourmet meals are served by reservation. Breakfast includes home-baked breads, jams, and jellies.

Less than a mile away is Hilltop Bed and Breakfast where you can use Theresa and Merle Kenkel's patio and grill, walk around the farm and look at the animals, relax in the hot tub, and enjoy a full country breakfast the next morning. Missouri Valley Antique Mall features furniture, quilts, china, and collectibles offered by sixty dealers. If you want to see more antiques, head to Logan to the Logan Antique Mall, 114 South Third Avenue. From Missouri Valley, head north on State 183,

Western central Iowa is apple country

passing the 155 acres of wildlife habitat at Sawmill Hollow. Head west on State 127 toward Mondamin (MON-da-min), the Winnebago name for corn.

Just west of Magnolia, you can drive the Orchard Ridge Loop through the loess hills orchards. Harrison County has more square acres planted to apple orchards than any other county in the state. The fruit is processed for wholesale distribution at the apple growers' cooperative packing facility in Woodbine. Some of the most popular types of apples are Jonathan, red and yellow Delicious, and Prairie Spy. Several orchards cater to visitors by providing U-pick facilities, selling apple cider and other apple products, and offering tours for groups.

Small's Fruit Farm, owned by Joyce and Russell Small, has been in the family since 1895. "Russell's grandfather bought some apples from a local farmer in 1894," explained Joyce. "They tasted so good that he returned the following year, bought the farmer's land, and planted an apple orchard." It was the first commercial orchard in the area. Today, the Smalls have seventy acres of orchards growing twenty to twenty-five varieties of apples. They sell apples, sparkling cider, apple butter, preserves, pickles, corncob jelly, nuts, and popcorn. The kids guzzled cups of apple cider and bought some apple butter to take home. Backtrack and head north on State 183.

The Loess Hills State Forest is along State 183, and plans call for it eventually to be more than 17,000 acres. Just west of Pisgah is Murray Hill. Charles Larpenteur, well-known French fur trader, lived in the area and was buried in the cemetery at Fountainbleu, also known as Murray Hill. The cemetery is at the foot of Murray Hill Road. Signs direct you to a scenic overlook on the road. From Pisgah, take County F20L across country to Woodbine.

Woodbine was named by an early resident for the flowering vine that grew near her home in England. Part of the original Lincoln Highway (US 30) runs the length of town. At

Eleventh and Par Streets, White's Floral Garden takes up most of a city block. The park was given to the town by Herbert White, a naturalist and botanist. The gardens contain many varieties of peonies, including some of White's hybrids existing only in these gardens, as well as unusual flowers, vines, shrubs, and trees. Continue north on US 30 to Dunlap.

If you are traveling in December, don't miss the town of Dunlap's Wax Nativity. It was started in 1951 when a local resident crafted the first wax figure. Over the years, more life-size figures, wearing human hair and dressed in real clothes, were created. Take US 30 through Dunlap, turn west on State 37 for a mile, and take the first right onto a country road, which leads you to the Nativity. At various times, carolers perform here. Continue northeast on US 30 to Dow City.

The brick S. E. Dow House on South Prince Street, built in 1872, is an example of homes of prominent, upper-class families. The house cost $11,000 to build, a pittance now, but at the time, most houses cost only $2,000. At one time, Dow owned 2,600 acres farmed by tenants. Simeon and Chloe Dow arrived in Crawford County in 1855 with their daughter, Alma, and a herd of cattle. They spent their first year in a log house only twelve by fourteen feet. The next year Dow introduced registered shorthorn cattle to the area and built a large log house, the family home for twenty years. Dow was not only a farmer, landlord, and stockman; he founded Dow City and served his community. He helped build the first schoolhouse, and opened his home for church services and a post office. Construction of the mansion on the hill began in 1872 and finished two years later. The Dows sold this home in 1902 and moved into town.

The mansion sat on a hill overlooking most of Dow's land holdings. The house was unusual in that it had the same floor plan on all three floors. The walls are three bricks wide, starting in the basement and extending up to support the roof. This home, like the earlier one, was open to weary travelers, who could sleep overnight, eat a good meal, and even get a fresh horse in the morning. Continue north on US 30 to Denison.

The Donna Reed Festival and Artist Workshops, a hometown tribute to the late actress who won an Oscar for her performance in *From Here to Eternity*, is held early in June. The festival usually includes a celebrity golf tournament, parade, air displays, stage performances, bike ride, and street fair. Workshops include acting, writing, music, production, directing, radio work, performing by persons with disabilities, and performing for disabled persons.

The McHenry House was built by W. A. McHenry, a Civil War veteran, banker, abstractor, cattleman, and early settler in Denison. In 1885 it cost him $24,000. The house, at Fifteenth Street and First Avenue North, contained fourteen rooms, hand-rubbed woodwork made of five different woods, and a third-floor ballroom with moveable stage. The house featured steam heat, pipes for hot and cold water, and speaking tubes in nearly every room, and was lighted by gas made on the premises. The third story had a maple floor and stained glass windows and was used for entertaining large groups. The Crawford County Historical Society hosts a Christmas gala each year in the Victorian home.

Nearby is the Abraham Lincoln farm site. Lincoln captained a militia company in the Black Hawk War of 1831–32. As a bonus, he received forty acres of land in Crawford County, but he never saw the land. His family sold it after his death. Highway markers on State 39 and State 59 northwest of Denison direct the way to the land. Continue north on State 39 to Odebolt. Drive six miles north and .25 miles west of Odebolt to Prairie Peddler.

The Peterson Pioneer House, 413 South Walnut Street, is considered to be the oldest dwelling in town. Nels Magnus Peterson and his wife Mary completed the one-and-one-half-story home in 1886. They reared their family of five children in the small, wood-frame house. Nels and Mary died in the early 1900s, and the last person to live in the house was their daughter Edith. The city took possession of the house for back taxes, but allowed her to continue to live there until her death in 1973. City elders decided to preserve the house, as it is considered to be an excellent example of pioneer architecture. Unlike many historic homes that have been preserved to show the lifestyle of wealthy families, this depicts the life of the common, working pioneers.

Another home to visit in Odebolt is Stuga, the Old Swedish House, at 700 Locust Street, adjacent to Faith Lutheran Church. John Nelson, a prominent resident of Odebolt, remembered his childhood home in Minnesota. He searched and found the small house, where he had lived with his parents and five siblings, and moved it to his farm outside Odebolt. The town inherited Stuga, the architecture of which had been copied from houses in the Swedish countryside, after John Nelson died. City elders moved the little house to its present location. "It's amazing that a family of seven lived in that little house," said Pastor Vic of the Lutheran Church. "It's just one room, about twelve by fourteen feet, with a loft, rock chimney, and a fireplace area." Parishioners helped in the restoration process. Visitors are asked to phone ahead to the church to arrange to visit Stuga.

Jane and Jack Hogue started Prairie Peddler when Jack's parents moved from the farm to town. Jane and her husband had lived in a trailer on the property and then moved into the farmhouse. "We had cement work in so many spots, I said to Jack, 'We should really have a garden.' " That was in 1979. Neither had much of a horticulture background. "Over the years as the gardens have stretched and expanded, we've developed some theme gardens," she explained. There is a garden of edible flowers, a calendar garden (a flower for every month of the year), a hummingbird garden (all red), fragrant garden, children's garden, annual drying garden, and perennial drying garden. Formal herb gardens include culinary bed, tussie mussie bed, medicinal herbs, and insect chasers. The moon garden contains only white fragrant flowers to be enjoyed in the evening. The moonvine, moonflower, false baby's breath, obedient flower, candytuft, feverfew, and nicotiana are planted in a crescent-shaped plot.

Jane's three children, ten, fourteen, and fifteen (in 1994) have picked a theme garden to care for. The oldest daughter has the secret garden, an enclosed garden. Her son pulls weeds in his barnyard garden, where all the plants have names of farm animals, such as lamb's ear, and hen and chicks. Emily, the youngest, started her garden when she was in preschool, and it is called the Kindergarden, with a flower for every letter of the alphabet.

In 1985 Jane opened her shop in a weathered chicken coop. "It took eight years for us to decide that it was a business," she laughed. Hundreds of dried flowers hang from the rafters. As glints of light pour in through cracks in the roof, you gaze up at an upside-down rainbow—rows of red roses and peonies, maroon and purple statice, bright yellow sunflowers, and purple lavender. Perhaps it's just the sun setting on another trip along country roads.

In the Area

Phone ahead as several attractions are open only seasonally.

DeSoto Visitors Center (Missouri Valley): 712-642-4121

Harrison County Museum and Iowa Welcome Center (Missouri Valley): 712-642-2114

Apple Orchard Inn Bed and Breakfast (Missouri Valley): 712-642-2418

Hilltop Bed and Breakfast (Missouri Valley): 712-642-3695

Missouri Valley Antique Mall (Missouri Valley): 712-642-2125

Logan Antique Mall (Missouri Valley): 712-644-2781

Small's Fruit Farm (Mondamin): 712-646-2723

White's Floral Garden (Woodbine): 712-647-2550

Wax Nativity (Dunlap): 712-643-5721

Dow House (Dow City): 712-674-3734

Donna Reed Festival and Artist Workshops (Denison): 712-263-5621

McHenry House (Denison): 712-263-3806

Peterson Pioneer House (Odebolt): 712-668-2231

Prairie Peddler (Odebolt): 712-668-4840

Stuga (Old Swedish House) (Odebolt): 712-668-4516

Index

FARMS and GARDENS (*cont.*)
  Dubuque Arboretum/Botanical
    Gardens, Dubuque, 67
  Eagle Point Nature Center,
    Clinton, 80
  Farm Park, Decorah, 28
  Garden Walk at Cothart Cottage,
    Davenport, 76–77
  Heard Gardens, Johnston, 126–127
  Heritage Farm, Decorah, 29–30
  Howell Tree Farm, Cumming, 130
  Iowa Arboretum, Madrid, 126
  Klokkenspiel garden, Pella,
    119–120
  Earl May Show Gardens,
    Shenandoah, 140
  New Melleray Abbey garden, 88
  Orchard Ridge Loop, 148
  Perennial Paradise, Postville, 42
  Pocket Seed Perennials, McGregor,
    36
  Prairie Peddler, Odebolt, 151–152
  Scholte House, Pella, 119
  Small's Fruit Farm, Mondamin, 148
  State Center Rose Garden, State
    Center, 113–114
  Sugarbush Farms, Frankville, 29
  White's Floral Garden, Woodbine,
    149
FESTIVALS
  Bald Eagle Appreciation Days,
    Keokuk, 100
  Black Dirt Days, Conrad, 113
  Bluegrass and Old-Time Country
    Music Festival, Stratford, 4
  Civil War Muster and Mercantile
    Exposition, East Davenport
    village, 76
  Country Music Festival, Garber, 69
  Covered Bridge Festival,
    Winterset, 131
  Dvorak Festival, Spillville, 23
  Eagle Grove Auction Barn,
    Goldfield, 11
  Fort Atkinson Rendezvous, Fort
    Atkinson, 23
  Frontier Days, Fort Dodge, 6–7
  German Fest, Guttenberg, 72
  Homecoming, Elgin, 50
  Midwest Old Threshers Reunion,
    Mount Pleasant, 93–95

  Glenn Miller Festival, Clarinda,
    141
  National Farm Toy Show,
    Dyersville, 61
  Nordic Fest, Decorah, 24–25
  Oktoberfest, St. Donatus, 88
  Old-Time Power Show, Garber,
    69–70
  Donna Reed Festival and Artist
    Workshops, Denison, 150
  Rose Festival, State Center, 114
  Sidney Rodeo, Sidney, 142
  Southwest Iowa Professional Hot
    Air Balloon Races, Creston, 137
  St. Boniface Labor day picnic, New
    Vienna, 64
  Summer Toy Festival, Dyersville,
    60–61
  Syttende Mai, Clermont, 50
  Tama Pow Wow, Tama, 114
  Tulip Festival, Pella, 117, 120
  Wax Nativity, Dunlap, 149
  Laura Ingalls Wilder Days, Burr
    Oak, 30

GALLERIES and MUSEUMS
  Adams County House of History,
    Corning, 138
  Apple Trees Museum, Burlington,
    108
  Arts for Living Center, Burlington,
    107
  Becker Woodcarving Museum,
    Dyersville, 63
  Bertrand Museum, Missouri Valley,
    145–146
  Bily Brothers Clocks, Spillville, 23
  Blanden Memorial Art Museum,
    Fort Dodge, 7
  Boone County Cultural Center and
    Historical Museum, Boone,
    124–126
  Boone County Museum, Boone,
    126
  Brunnier Gallery and Museum,
    Ames, 123
  Buffalo Bill Museum, LeClaire, 77
  Carter House Museum, Elkader,
    47
  Clarinda Mental Health Institution
    Museum, Clarinda, 141

156

Index

Index

Iowa Capitol Building, Des
  Moines, 128
Ironclad Store, Froelich, 42
Jordan House, West Des Moines,
  129
Lee County Courthouse, Fort
  Madison, 103
Henderson Lewelling house,
  Salem, 95
Locust School, Decorah, 28
Lourdes Catholic Church,
  Waukon, 40
Madison County Courthouse,
  Winterset, 131
Mamrelund Lutheran Church,
  Stanton, 139
McHenry House, Denison, 150
Samuel F. Miller House, Keokuk,
  100
Montauk, Clermont, 50–51
Montgomery County Courthouse,
  Red Oak, 139
Motor Mill, Motor, 53, 73
Old Elkader Opera House,
  Elkader, 48–49
Old Fort Madison, Fort Madison,
  102
Old Main elementary school,
  Stanton, 139
Opera House, Volga, 54
Pearson House, Keosauqua, 97
Peterson Pioneer House, Odebolt,
  150–151
Phelph House, Burlington, 107–108
Plagman Barn, Garber, 69–70
Reburn twelve-sided barn, New
  Albin, 40
Redstone Inn, Dubuque, 68
Salisbury House, Des Moines,
  127–128
Scholte House, Pella, 119
Schoolhouse and sod house, West
  Bend, 8
Sherman Hill Historic District, Des
  Moines, 128–129
St. Boniface Church, New Vienna,
  64
St. Donatus Church and Pieta
  Chapel, St. Donatus, 86
St. Francis Xavier Basilica,
  Dyersville, 62–63

St. Joseph's Catholic Church,
  Elkader, 49
St. Luke's United Methodist
  Church, Dubuque, 68
St. Peter and Paul's Church, West
  Bend, 10
St. Wenceslaus Church, Spillville,
  23
Stone School, Lansing, 39
Strawtown buildings, Pella, 117
Stuga (Old Swedish House),
  Odebolt, 151
Terrace Hill, Des Moines, 129
Union Sunday School, Clermont,
  51
Van Allen Building, Clinton, 79
Van Buren County Courthouse,
  Keosauqua, 97–98
Villa Louis, Prairie du Chien,
  Wisconsin, 36
Wabash Depot, Shenandoah, 140
Walnut Grove Pioneer Village,
  Long Grove, 78–79
West Jefferson Street, Burlington,
  106
West Pleasant Street Historic
  District, Maquoketa, 82
Wiemerslage farmstead barn, New
  Albin, 40
HISTORIC SITES
  Battle of Bad Ax, Black Hawk Bluff,
    40
  Dunning's Spring, Decorah, 26
  Effigy Mounds National
    Monument, Marquette, 37–38
  Ely Ford, Keosauqua, 97
  Fish Farm Mounds, New Albin,
    39–40
  Grotto of the Redemption, West
    Bend, 9–10
  Hawkeye Log Cabin, Burlington,
    108
  Hurstville Lime Kilns, Maquoketa,
    83
  Jonas Jones house, Tabor, 142
  Chief Keokuk burial site, Keokuk,
    101
  Klokkenspiel, Pella, 119–120
  Abraham Lincoln farm site,
    Denison, 150
  National Cemetery, Keokuk, 99

159

Index

Shimek State Forest, Farmington,
   99
Siewer Springs State Trout Rearing
   Station, Decorah, 28–29
South Sabula Lakes Park, Sabula,
   80–81
Spook Cave, McGregor, 42–44
Upper Iowa River, 24
Volga River State Park, Fayette, 21
Wabash Trace Nature Trail,
   Shenandoah, 140
Yellow River State Forest, 38

PLANES. *See* BOATS, PLANES and
   TRAINS

SHOPS and MARKETS
   Clesne Coast-to-Coast Store,
      Elkader, 48
   Conrad General Store, Conrad,
      112–113
   Country Crafts, Stratford, 4
   Country Cupboard, Bellevue, 85
   Country Store, Pella, 117
   Dakota Shop, Goldfield, 11
   Dows Mercantile, Dows, 12
   Eldorado Store, Eldorado, 22
   Elkader General Store, Elkader, 48
   Farmer's Market, Dubuque, 68
   Farmer's Market, Guttenberg,
      71–72
   The Fiber Shop, Davenport, 76
   Ben Franklin store, Pella, 119
   Gardini's General Store, Lehigh,
      4–5
   Glass and Gifts, Stratford, 4
   Goldfield Cheese Mart and Gift
      Shop, Goldfield, 11
   Gonners Store, Springbrook, 83
   Greef General Store, Bentonsport,
      97
   Harbor Place Mall, Dubuque, 67
   Neil Hershberger's, Oelwein, 19
   In't Veld Meat Market, Pella, 119
   Iron & Lace blacksmith/pottery
      shop, Bentonsport, 97
   Jaarsma Bakery, Pella, 119
   Mary Anne Keppler's Country
      Calico, Gunder, 53
   Kerper's Country Store, New
      Vienna, 63–64

Klompenshop, Pella, 120
Lu's Glass Art, Stratford, 4
Make Mine Country, Fort Dodge, 7
Marlyne's Palettable Gifts, Conrad,
   113
Miller's Country Store, Oelwein,
   20
Millstone Emporium, Postville, 42
Monk Fish Market, Waukon, 38
New Melleray Abbey, 88
Pine Grove Store, Oelwein, 19–20
Stone Balloon Book Store,
   McGregor, 34
Tomorrow's Keepsakes, Bellevue,
   85
Toy Farmer Country Store,
   Dyersville, 61
Troll House, Stanton, 139
Vande Lune Fabrics, Pella, 119
Vander Ploegs bakery, Pella, 119
White Fox Gift Shop, Clarion, 12
Laura Yutzy's, Oelwein, 18–19

TEA ROOMS and TAVERNS
   Alpha's, Fort Madison, 103
   Blue Willow Tea Room and Bakery,
      Harcourt, 5
   Bonaparte's Retreat, Bonaparte, 98
   Breitbach's Country Dining,
      Balltown, 68–69
   Briar Patch Tea Room, Conrad, 112
   Cafe Deluxe, Decorah, 26
   Liz Clark's, Keokuk, 101
   Cliff House, Decorah, 27
   Country Inn, Conrad, 112
   Country Junction, Dyersville, 61
   Dakota Shop, Goldfield, 11
   Dayton House, Decorah, 27
   Elkader General Store, Elkader, 48
   In Good Company, Stratford, 4
   Kaffe Stuga, Swedesburg, 92
   Kalmes Restaurant and Olde
      Tavern, St. Donatus, 88
   Keystone Restaurant, Patio, and
      Saloon, Elkader, 48
   La Corsette, Newton, 116
   Landmark Inn, Waukon, 40
   LeWright's Locker, Goldfield, 11
   Potter's Mill, Bellevue, 84
   Sampler House Tea Room,
      Keokuk, 101

161

Country Roads of Iowa

162

Index

Other titles in the Country Roads series:

Country Roads of Connecticut and Rhode Island
Country Roads of Florida
Country Roads of Hawaii
Country Roads of Illinois, second edition
Country Roads of Indiana
Country Roads of Kentucky
Country Roads of the Maritimes
Country Roads of Massachusetts
Country Roads of Michigan, second edition
Country Roads of New Jersey
Country Roads of New Hampshire
Country Roads of New York
Country Days in New York City
Country Roads of North Carolina
Country Roads of Ohio
Country Roads of Ontario
Country Roads of Oregon
Country Roads of Pennsylvania
Country Roads of Tennessee
Country Roads of Vermont
Country Roads of Virginia
Country Roads of Washington

All books are $9.95 at bookstores.
Or order directly from the publisher (add $3.00
shipping & handling for direct orders):

Country Roads Press
P.O. Box 286
Castine, Maine 04421
Toll-free phone number: **800-729-9179**